PUFFIN BOOKS

MYTHONAMA: THE BIG BOOK OF INDIAN MYTHOLOGIES

We speak so many languages. Be it music or mathematics, football or baking, birdwatching, coding, painting, rapping, pretty much everything has a code, a common language.

Mudita loves the idea of language, how we can immerse ourselves in it and then use it in countless creative ways. She trained as a journalist but found her true calling in the world of publishing as an editor—a wonderful profession where her OCDs become her USPs! **Adittya** learnt the language of design as an architect, but found that life had other designs for him, when his passion for quizzing inevitably became his profession.

Together, they have crossed many milestones, from turning entrepreneurs to becoming parents, speaking different languages to fulfil different roles. The common language that has united them and all their works, however, has been that of curiosity. The joy of discovery, of sharing with others the wonder of exploration is now their vocabulary for personal and professional fulfilment.

Mudita and Adittya live and work in New Delhi, sharing their lives with their children, Shireen Saudamini, Noor Vasundhara and Sushi the beagle. Together, they manage Quizcraft Global, a knowledge solutions enterprise, and together they hope to create more while aspiring towards a language of wisdom.

CONTENTS

A NOTE FROM THE AUTHORS

A story can be so many things. A joke that makes you giggle till your sides hurt or a tragic tale that makes you weep. It can stump you with an unanswered question or enlighten you with a life lesson. A heroic ballad or a pithy parable, it can entertain you, mystify you, irritate you or, well, bore you! As long as there have been people, as long as there will be people, as long as there are thoughts, there will be stories. And that's what myths are. Stories of old, very old times and people and events, told and retold by people like you and us, generation after generation, civilization after civilization.

Like a fairy tale, a myth may begin with 'Once upon a time . . .', but may not always end with 'And they lived happily ever after'. Often, it is a mystery how a myth began. Then, there are multiple versions of the same myth. Siblings from one legend may be friends in another or spouses in a third! This is because myths are narrated or written by different people in different circumstances to explain different situations, perhaps to different audiences. Whether factual or fictional, myths are clearly persistent. From legendary stories of epics like the Avesta, Quran or Mahabharata to brand icons like Medusa of Versace or Hanuman of Maruti, myths are all around us. And, like stories, myths are many things.

It is said that Krishna spoke the entire Gita (yes, hundreds and hundreds of verses!) on the battlefield of Kurukshetra to inspire Arjuna. You may believe this, or not, but if you read it, you will find many tips that will guide you in school, at home, in an inter-school match, in dealing with your siblings, in an examination, in how you speak with people and how you use social media! The trick is to see through the myth and find its core idea: friendship or loyalty, business and sportsmanship, good versus evil, caring for animals or perhaps even sustainability and conservation of resources.

Be it the Bible, the Torah or the Guru Granth Sahib; shlokas in the Vedas or Hadith in the Quran; agamas and sutras of Jainism and Buddhism; or the countless stories in cults, clans and communities, treasure troves of tales are waiting to be heard, dissected, interpreted, reimagined, retold . . . to perpetuate the process of myth-making, of which we are all a part.

So, let's dive right into the ocean of legends from India's many mythologies. Remember, mythology does not equal religion. Characters, places and events in myths are as 'sacred' as they are 'secular'; they represent ideas that transcend ideologies. Let us time-travel with them, let us learn about fantastic beasts and mind-boggling weapons, but let us also open our minds and hearts to the gems of knowledge in these myths.

Through anecdotes, fables, quizzes, crosswords, illustrations and other activities, this book brings to you but a fraction of the fathomless mythology of this land. We hope you enjoy reading and learning this book, and that it sets you off on a wonderful journey of discovery.

1

FROM ZERO TO INFINITY

Creation Myths from around the World

*How did our universe begin?
When did it come into existence? Who made it?
Every civilization has creation myths to answer these
questions and tell us about the beginnings of Earth, life and
nature. Most start in similar ways—with stories or theories
on nothingness or chaos, often in a liquid state, from which
emerged gods, lands, humans, animals and more. Sometimes
such stories make it seem like it all came into being via primal
3D printing. You may find these tales funny, fantastical, even
incredible. You may relate them to theories like the big bang.
And you may even discover deeper meanings. And so we begin
our book—right from the start—by delving into creation myths.*

Then even nothingness was not, nor existence,
There was no air then, nor the heavens beyond it.
What covered it? Where was it? In whose keeping?
Was there then cosmic water, in depths unfathomed?

Then there was neither death nor immortality
nor was there then the torch of night and day.
The One breathed windlessly and self-sustaining.
There was that One then, and there was no other.

At first there was only darkness wrapped in darkness.
All this was only unillumined cosmic water.
That One which came to be, enclosed in nothing,
arose at last, born of the power of heat.

In the beginning desire descended on it—
that was the primal seed, born of the mind.
The sages who have searched their hearts with wisdom
know that which is kin to that which is not.

And they have stretched their cord across the void,
and know what was above, and what below.
Seminal powers made fertile mighty forces.
Below was strength, and over it was impulse.

But, after all, who knows, and who can say
Whence it all came, and how creation happened?
The gods themselves are later than creation,
so who knows truly whence it has arisen?

Whence all creation had its origin,
the creator, whether he fashioned it or whether he did not,
the creator, who surveys it all from highest heaven,
he knows—or maybe even he does not know.

This is Indologist A.L. Basham's well-known interpretation of the Rig Veda's 'Nasadiya Sukta', also called the 'Hymn of Creation'. If you read it carefully, you'll notice that it does not use religious words or symbols. So, even though it appears in a Hindu scripture, it is almost unreligious or agnostic in character. Due to its objective nature, it has been appreciated and interpreted by people across the world, from astronomer Carl Sagan to film-maker Shyam Benegal. And we would like to use it to begin this book and this interaction with you as we dive into the legends of how everything was created.

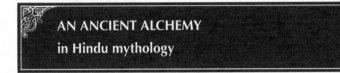

AN ANCIENT ALCHEMY
in Hindu mythology

Let us study the above chant from the perspective of Hindu mythology. Um, make that one of *many* perspectives, actually! We could say that first there was, well, nothing. But it isn't easy to imagine how neither something nor nothing existed. What is nothing? In fact, what is nothing without something?

And so, slowly, over a long time, did come Something. The life force stirred. Perhaps then emerged a tiny golden egg, Hiranyagarbha, the 'universal germ'. It appeared on its own, out of nothingness, holding within itself the 'essence' of creation. It has been called Brahman, the 'soul of the universe', which floated about in the emptiness of non-existence for a year, then divided into halves to form Prithvi and Swarga (Earth and heaven). In some accounts, Hiranyagarbha is also said to be Vishnu, the Creator itself, asleep like an embryo.

3

When Vishnu awoke, it became Brahma, and creation happened, just like that. In a spontaneous burst of cosmic energy, like foam on the waves of the ocean, were born light, sound, heat, land, sea, sky, plant, animal, human. One by one, they came into being and populated the space of creation. Faith meets science? Food for thought.

The concept of time in Hinduism, quite like in Buddhism and Jainism, is cyclical—going round and round like the wheels of a cycle. Whatever is will, one day, not be. What is born will die. Over time, these creatures that came into being will perish. All will end. Vishnu, who became Brahma, will become Shiva, and destroy it all. Then destroy itself. And then, once again, there will be nothingness. For a long time, *shunya, sifr*. And then the cycle will repeat . . .

That was the story of creation in a nutshell. It becomes more interesting when one dives deeper. Who was Vishnu? Where was he? How did Brahma awake? What did he create first?

Read more about this in 'A Leaf of Faith', page 139.

It is believed that he first created the gods, then the demons, then animals and humans, and so on. When it came to the human race, it was first the sages born from his mind, then the kings who emerged from his arms, then the traders who shrugged out of his thighs and finally, the workers who squeezed out of his feet. How the caste system thus came into being and how everyone knew 'their place' in society: that is a discussion for another time and book.

THE SOUND OF SILENCE?

The one thing you must remember about mythology is that there is no one myth. The very nature of a myth is nonfactual, since it is based in legend, belief and faith, and hence, there are many versions of the same event or entity. So is it with the myth of creation. Different sources will give you different interpretations of creation. You will hear of the formless Swayambhu, who assumed the form of the golden egg. Narayana, Ishwar and Brahman will appear as the origin and end of all creation, quite like the multi-headed, multi-eyed, multi-footed, multi-armed, multi-limbed, multi-dimensional Hari.

There are also the twin balancing forces of Purusha, who acts, and Prakriti, who evolves, together generating the universe. Then there is Prajapati, described in many ways in scripture, from the 'lord of all born beings' to a sort of mother goddess to a divine stag. In the 'Hiranyagarbha Sukta' of the Rig Veda, Prajapati is the creator deity, 'God of gods'. In the Yajur Veda, the sounds he emitted became the sky, Earth and seasons. When he inhaled, he created gods, fire and light; when he exhaled, demons and darkness. Then, he co-created the world with Vach, the goddess of language. He uttered the potent trinity of words—*bhu bhuvah svaha*—a few times. Uttering bhu, Prajapati made the earth, uttering bhuvah, he made air, and uttering svaha, he made the sky. Then, repeating the three words, he made Brahmin, Kshatriya, Vaishya. And finally, he renewed himself, created his offspring, then animals.

THE LIGHTNESS OF BEING
in Buddhist mythology

The world, as Buddha described it in a discourse recorded in the *Aggañña Sutta*, came into being when the earth and stars spontaneously formed on their own in the vast stillness of nothingness. Water and air collected and merged to become streams, rivers, lakes and oceans on Earth. But life did not yet exist.

Then gradually appeared beings, composed of pristine light and pure energy. Formless and ageless, but not directionless. They hyper jumped through space, frequency hopped through time . . . until they tasted the sweet earth. And bodies formed. Slowly, they became coarser and more textured, both in body and mind. These became men and women, who populated Earth. But their minds slowly became used to sloth, and they battled with each other over food, land, water and other material things. Thus was created war, misery, laziness, hunger and avarice. Welcome to the world as we know it!

According to the Buddha, Earth was created during one cycle of expansion and contraction of the universe. And it will disappear—*poof!*—in the next such cycle. To start over again . . . Remember the cycle of time? Beyond such nuggets of information, the Buddha wasn't too keen on discussions regarding the origins of the world, since he felt that the past didn't really matter. What mattered was what humans did in the world, in the present. And that is why this is the most common refrain in the *Aggañña Sutta*:

Dhamma is the best thing for people
In this life and the next as well

MIGHT OF THE MAKER
in Islamic mythology

According to the Quran, in the beginning, heaven and Earth were one. Allah split them into two with a loud sound (the big bang?), but also commanded them to stay together forever and abide by the laws of nature, his laws. There lies nothing between God and creation, so believe Muslims. *Kun fayakun.* 'Be,' commands he, and it is.

He formed all celestial bodies and created their orbits so that they are never still and never lost. He shaped the earth with its mountains and seas, islands and forests. He studded the night with stars and the moon. He brightened the day with the blazing sun. His act of creating and ordering the universe is the act of prime mercy, for which all things sing his glories. Allah is present in everything, but not embodied or incarnated in anything.

Allah created the universe in six days, it is said. In various verses, the word *yawm* (meaning 'day') implies different time periods, some as long as 50,000 years. Basically, it is not a day, but an era, which is why the six-day creation can be interpreted as six distinct periods or aeons, or what we could also perhaps call evolution. Also in keeping with scientific theories is the Quran's belief that 'Allah has created every animal from water . . . some that creep on their bellies, some that walk on two legs and some that walk on four'. However, you'll find a deviation from the theory of evolution in Islamic belief as it does not accept the descent of man from apes. Allah created Adam and Hawwa (or Eve), as we are today, from clay. He sculpted humans, moulded them and breathed life into them.

On the seventh 'day', he ascended his throne and probably sat back to admire his handiwork: life. Or perhaps added some final touches, a pair of fins here, some flowers there. For the work of creation, you see, is never done. Each new child, every seed that sprouts into a sapling, every new species is part of the process. It goes on until it is time for it to be destroyed.

A CREATIVE APPROACH
in Sikh mythology

Approaching the subject rather practically, Sikhism fast-forwards through the creation backstory. The *Guru Granth Sahib* dedicates more energy and text to the wonder of God's creation than to its possible origins. Referring to the idea of creation, it says:

'What was that time, and what was that moment?

What was that day, and what was that date?

What was that season, and what was that month,

when the Universe was created?

The Pandits, the religious scholars, cannot find that

time, even if it is written in the Puraanas.

That time is not known to the Qazis,

who study the Koran.

The day and the date are not known to the Yogis,

nor is the month or the season.

The Creator who created this creation—only He

Himself knows.'

Instead of focusing on the when, how and why of creation, Sikh gurus teach us the importance of respecting and sustaining creation. The purpose of human life, they say, is to create harmony with everything around us: birds, animals, trees, flowers and other people.

HEART OF LIGHT
in Zoroastrian mythology

The core Zoroastrian myth has been the battle between good and evil. Between Ormazd (Ahura Mazda) and Ahriman. White and black. Light and dark. In Avestan texts, in the beginning, Ormazd lived in pure light, Ahriman dwelt in deep darkness and between them was the void, nothingness. Creation began when O cast a beam of light into the void and shaped his creations as 'bright, white fire', a spiritual state in which they stayed for 3000 years. Meanwhile, A fashioned demonic creatures out of darkness and attacked the luminous world, rejecting all offers of peace. Angels called *yazatas* fought with O, while A had the support of *daevas* and *dregvants*. They fought for 9000 years until O managed to knock out A for 3000 years. In that time, creation occurred in the material realm.

First came the sky, encasing the world like an eggshell; then water within the egg; then earth floating on water; then plant, bull and the first man, Gayomart; and finally, fire. To protect the creations were seven beneficent immortals, the *amesha spentas*.

9

THE MYTH OF NON-CREATION
in Jain mythology

Jainism, interestingly, has no creation legends. In fact, this non-theistic religion has a non-creation myth, found in the ninth century CE text *Mahapurana* by Jain scholar Jinasena. Famously, and a bit brazenly, he says: 'Some foolish men declare that a Creator made the world . . . If God created the world, where was he before the creation? If he was transcendent then and needed no support, where is he now? How could God have made this world without any raw material?' He questions why God created evil at all. Fair point. So, the Jains firmly believe that the universe was never created. It always was, and always will be. In this uncreated and eternal world, there are *jivas* (living souls) and *ajivas* (non-living objects). Since nothing is destroyed or created, it simply changes from one form to another. The world just keeps going by its own energy processes. Are you thinking about the first law of thermodynamics?

Jains also live by the concept of karma, less in the spiritual sense of Hindus and Buddhists, and more in the metaphysical sense in which karma is actually karmic matter that collects on one's soul because of one's actions. Think of it as a bookshelf collecting dust. Once this attachment happens, the soul needs to discard it and thereby, it gets stuck in the karmic cycle of birth, death, rebirth, repeat. With no god to turn to, it is up to us to release our souls from this samsara and attain moksha. To help us along, there are the five vows: ahimsa (non-violence), satya (truthfulness), *asteya* (integrity), *brahmacharya* (faithfulness) and *aparigraha* (non-attachment). Tough ask? Which is why only the people who achieve moksha during their lifetime are called Jinas ('those who overcome'), and that elusive word gives this religion its name.

Let's get creative with creation and non-creation, shall we? Decipher these clues to arrive at the words hidden in the grid, locate them, mark them out and you can attain maze moksha!

W	A	Y	A	M	E	L	O	H	I	M	T	A
S	A	M	S	A	R	A	M	A	E	O	H	H
W	O	G	A	Y	O	M	A	R	T	U	M	R
A	L	O	Y	H	A	V	W	O	N	N	Z	I
Y	G	L	W	O	R	F	L	A	V	T	B	N
A	N	D	B	S	H	I	V	A	G	A	P	A
M	E	E	H	R	N	A	M	H	A	R	B	M
B	Q	N	U	A	I	R	D	A	R	A	H	S
H	H	X	C	R	T	E	W	T	N	F	Z	A
U	F	E	Y	N	S	I	H	Q	E	A	C	T
Z	I	A	W	W	A	H	H	W	W	T	Z	A
A	M	A	N	H	A	R	B	S	A	M	H	Z
N	A	S	A	D	I	Y	A	S	U	K	T	A
U	R	U	G	E	H	A	W	A	D	T	M	Y

CLUES

1. First man in creation and the first king in Iranian mythical history as per Avestan legend (8)
2. The first woman created by Allah, according to the Quran (5)
3. The hill outside Mecca where the first man and first woman reunited after they were sent to the earth (5,6)

4. When Vishnu becomes this form of power, the Destroyer, he will end creation so it can begin again (5)

5. The prime evil spirit of darkness in the Zoroastrian creation myth; also called Angra Mainyu (7)

6. In Jainism, the continuous cycle of rebirths and reincarnations, from which moksha is the only way out (7)

7. Of the many names of God in Gurmukhi, this one that means 'wonderful lord' is the most common; also a gurmantra (8)

8. Ahura Mazda's angels who fight Ahriman's forces; they pour sunlight on Earth to help man (7)

9. Literally 'self-manifested', this is a name by which Brahma was known, because he created himself (9)

10. Colour of the cosmic egg, floating on a sea of nothingness and splitting to create the universe (6)

11. Hebrew God, whose personal name was revealed to Moses as YHWH or Yahweh (6)

12. Sacred prayer with which Ahriman's first attack was overcome by Ormazd (5,6)

13. In Hinduism, the divine and universal force underlying all reality or, perhaps, reality itself (7)

14. The 129th hymn of the tenth mandala of the Rig Veda; the 'Hymn of Creation' (8,5)

15. The 'heaven of satisfaction' where the future Buddha Maitreya waits to be born on Earth

2

GODS OF ALL THINGS

Major and Minor Deities

While men (and women) live their lives on Earth, they do look for guidance every now and then. And whom do they look to? Gods, of course. At first, we worshipped the forces of nature, mostly out of fear of their wrath, but as society grew more complex and technology advanced, they lost their fear of natural phenomena and created newer gods that were stronger and 'better' than the old ones. Some old ones were replaced, some just absorbed. Let's look at the span of deities in the very many pantheons.

 WHO'S WHO?

As you read these divine descriptions and imagine the lives of gods and goddesses, here's a challenge for you. This chapter is peppered with illustrations that are fully detailed but not labelled. You need to figure out who is who, and name the illustrations correctly!

THE HINDU PANTHEON

BRAHMA, the Creator, is said to have hatched from the golden egg Hiranyagarbha or emerged from a lotus growing out of Vishnu's navel. He is depicted with four heads—one for each of the Vedas, yugas, varnas, directions, basically anything counted in fours—but there's one hidden under his hair. It is said that this fifth one was once knocked off by Shiva, when Brahma was being too smart. The god of knowledge, Brahma, is probably responsible for granting more (ambiguous) boons than any other deity. Riding a white goose (or swan), he is accompanied by Saraswati and Savitri, the goddesses of wisdom and faithfulness.

SARASWATI was created by Brahma; some say as his daughter, some say his consort. Worshipped as the goddess of learning, she is not overly ornamented, which suggests her focus on spiritual, not material, wealth. Her *vahana* or divine vehicle is commonly a pristine white swan (also a goose at times) and she sits on it, holding a manuscript and playing the veena. All these elements symbolize her domain as that of the arts and learning. Earlier, Saraswati used to also be identified with the Vedic goddess of speech, Vach, and the vanished sacred river that shares her name. She is also credited for inventing the Sanskrit language.

VISHNU, the Preserver, lives in Vaikuntha, reclining on the mighty Sheshanaga. Generally shown as light blue in colour and four-armed, he holds a conch, a mace, a lotus bloom and the potent Sudarshana Chakra, his weapon of choice. Vishnu seldom loses his temper, doesn't normally get tricked and is the go-to guy whenever creation is threatened by demons or calamities. Over the yugas, he has made various appearances on Earth to combat evil. Frequently, he turns into the beautiful Mohini, who uses her feminine charms to get work done without violence. Negotiation skills on point!

Read all about Vishnu's avatars on page 25.

LAKSHMI, the consort of Vishnu—both in his omnipresent four-armed form as well as in his different avatars—arose from the depths of the Ocean of Milk when it was churned by the asuras and devas in their quest for amrit. Seated on a pink lotus, she showers blessings in the form of gold on her devotees and, in turn, is showered with milk or water by a pair of elephants. Lakshmi, along with Ganesha, is especially worshipped on Diwali with bhaktas asking her to bless them with wealth and their enterprises with success. Her vehicle is Ulooka, the owl.

SHIVA, the Destroyer, is also called the divine yogi. He dwells on Mount Kailasa with Parvati. They share such a close bond that they are sometimes worshipped as the unified Ardhanarishvara, half-Shiva, half-Parvati. He has the famous third eye that in a rage blasts to ashes, or into nothingness, anything he targets. He is also a giver of boons, generous to his worshippers. He caught the Ganga in his hair when she descended from the heavens and could have washed away the earth. With his monstrous-looking attendants called *ganas*, led by Ganesha the elephant god, Nandi the bull and Virbhadra the demon, he creates quite a spectacle when travelling.

PARVATI was not Shiva's first wife. That was Sati, who couldn't bear it when her father insulted her husband and promptly jumped into a sacrificial fire. Upon hearing this, an incensed Shiva went ballistic and destroyed half the world before Vishnu managed to calm him down. Sati was then reborn as Uma, or Parvati, daughter of the mountain god Himavan. After performing severe penance, she finally married Shiva. They had two children, the elephant god Ganesha and the warrior god Kartikeya.

DURGA, the warrior goddess, was the physical form of all powers of all gods, manifested to slay Mahishasura. But she is much more than the martial deity Rama worshipped with 108 blue lotuses before battling Ravana. She is the proto-deity Yogmaya, Vishnu's sister, who preserves the world while he sleeps. She took birth as Yashoda's child, replaced Krishna as Devaki's baby in jail, slipped out of Kamsa's grasp, assumed her celestial form and foretold his death.

Read more about this in 'Call of Deity: Legendary Warfare', page 170.

In Odisha's Jagannath Yatra, Jagannath (Krishna) is worshipped with his siblings Balabhadra (Balarama) and Subhadra. In some legends, Subhadra too is a manifestation of Yogmaya or Durga.

WHO AM I?

GANESHA was created by Parvati as her loyal sentinel. After all, Shiva had his ganas. So she animated a clay statue and allotted him sentry duty. Even Shiva couldn't get past him. In the ensuing fight, Shiva cut off his head, igniting Parvati's fury and compelling Brahma to make peace by giving the headless being an elephant head. Thus emerged Ganesha, the divine son. Leader of Shiva's cohorts, Ganesha is regarded as the favourite god to worship since he is

Read more about this mad dad in 'In the Name of the Father', page 203.

Vighnaharta, remover of obstacles and one who bestows good fortune. Ganesha is also very learned and wrote the Mahabharata on Veda Vyasa's dictation.

KARTIKEYA was born as the result of a prophecy that the son of Shiva would kill the demon Tarakasura. Kamadeva was sent to create an atmosphere conducive to the marriage of Shiva and Parvati, but got reduced to ashes for his trouble. Remember the third eye? However, the love god did accomplish his task and soon the warrior god Kartikeya, also known by names like Murugan, Skanda and Kumara, was born. Armed with his weapon, the Vel, he set out on his mission and destroyed Tarakasura. Along the way, he defeated the demon Soorapadman, who changed into a peacock and became his vahana.

ELEMENTAL DEITIES

INDRA, perhaps the most important god in the Vedic religion, was the protector of Kshatriyas. Thunderbolt-wielding and rain-giving, Indra was benevolent and generous to his worshippers, bringing them peace and prosperity. However, in later stories, Indra is not the all-powerful king of gods but is prone to human emotions like jealousy, anger, greed and hatred. In the Hindu creation myth, Indra was born from the mouth of a giant called Vishwapurusha, along with other devas who emerged from other body parts. These gods brought order to the cosmos and Indra became their ruler in Devaloka, along with his queen Indrani.

VAYU, god of air and wind, was one of the eight *dikpalas* (guardians of the—no, not galaxy—but directions; north-west in his case). As you can guess, Vayu was born of the *breath* of Vishwapurusha. He was one of the main triad of elemental gods of the Vedic period, and is sometimes also named Rudra. In the Puranic period, his importance waned, though he still remained one of the major devas, since he was responsible for all the breath that all living beings drew. He was the father of Hanuman and Bhima, and is shown riding a blackbuck.

WHO AM I? _____

AGNI, god of fire, is regarded as a friend of humanity. He exists in many forms: sun, lightning, comets, sacrificial fire, domestic fire, funeral pyre and the digestive fire inside us! More Vedic hymns have been dedicated to him than to any other deity, and he is still considered omnipresent, though not worshipped directly. Agni knows everyone's thoughts and witnesses everyone's actions, and is used in many important ceremonies, such as marriage. He is easily identified by his flaming hair and goat mount. He is also depicted with two heads, showing how fire can be beneficial as well as dangerous.

VARUNA, god of the hydrosphere—basically all water—was super important in the early Vedic period but, over time, was superseded by the trio of Indra, Agni and Vayu. He was relieved of some more duties by Sagara, god of seas and oceans, in the Puranic period. The dikpala of the west, he rides the fabulous makara and wields a noose as his weapon. He was the keeper of the Gandiva bow that was given to Arjuna during the Dwapara Yuga with its inexhaustible quivers of arrows. In earlier times, he was also identified—or twinned—with Mithra, dispenser of justice.

SURYA, the sun god, is son to Aditi and Kashyapa, son-in-law to the divine architect Vishwakarma and father to Yama, Yami, Shani and Karna. Riding a chariot pulled by seven horses and driven by Aruna, he brings light and life to the world. His importance can be gauged by the shlokas in the Vedas, Puranas and later epics that call him creator of life, dispeller of darkness, eye of the universe and soul of all existence. He is especially worshipped during Makar Sankranti, Pongal, Chhath Puja and Kumbh Mela, and has well-known temples in Modhera and Konark.

SOMA or **CHANDRA**, the moon god depicted as a beautiful young man, is one of the *navagrahas* (nine planets). He is the father of Budha (the planet Mercury) with Tara, though his main consort is Rohini, one of the twenty-seven daughters of Daksha. His appearance, like the moon, changes in different versions over time, but he is generally armed with a mace and rides a chariot with three wheels, or pulled by three horses. His enmity with Ganesha (over the modak incident) is the reason why it is said to be inauspicious (and forbidden) to look at the moon on Ganesha Chaturthi.

Read more about this in 'Call of Deity: Legendary Warfare', page 163.

Read more about this in 'Festivals of the Faraway Folk', page 220.

WHO AM I?

24

YAMA, god of death and dikpala of the south, is the son of Surya and Sanjana, and Yami's twin. Sadly, Sanjana left Surya—she couldn't stand his radiance—and, in her place, left Chhaya who mistreated the kids. When Yama called her out, she cursed

Read more about this in 'Binary Beings', page 93.

him to become lame. Overhearing this, Surya realized that his 'wife' wasn't his wife and reconciled with Sanjana. Part of the deal was that his dad-in-law Vishwakarma shaved off his radiance to obtain material to create amazing weapons like Vishnu's Sudarshana Chakra. Dark and fearsome, Yama rides a buffalo and captures souls with his noose.

DASHAVATARA: THE MANY FORMS OF VISHNU

In the Gita, Krishna tells Arjuna that whenever Dharma (which means 'goodness and good people') is in grave danger, he—whom we know is Vishnu—comes to Earth to protect it, as he is the Preserver of the cosmos. The order of these arrivals or avatars—nine, so far—somewhat echoes the evolutionary journey. Life began in the primal waters, and avatar #1 was a fish. Next came an amphibious turtle, then a feral boar, leading to a man-lion, a dwarf and then a set of Homo sapiens. The final avatar is one who we hope won't turn up too soon because he signals the end of the world as we know it.

#1 MATSYA THE FISH

In his earliest avatar, Vishnu came as a fish to rescue Manu and the *saptarishis* in the great flood and to recover the Vedas that the horse-headed Hayagriva had grabbed. Tiny fish Matsya appeared in the water that King Satyavrata was about to offer to the gods, asking for protection. The fish grew rapidly, outgrowing every container—*kamandalu*, water-pot, well, tank—till it was released into the sea. It told Satyavrata to find a pair of every species of living thing and put them into a boat and keep them safe from the great, world-ending flood that was on its way. (Noah's ark, anyone?) Meanwhile, he killed Hayagriva, recovered the Vedas, developed a horn on its head and returned with the serpent king Vasuki. Manu's ship with its precious cargo was tied to the horn, and they floated about till the flood ebbed and Earth could be repopulated.

#2 KURMA THE TORTOISE

You know how the devas and the asuras were continually battling, right? Once, when the devas were getting pummelled, they were advised to consume amrit, the nectar of immortality. To get it, they had to churn the Ocean of Milk. It wasn't an easy task, so they collaborated with the asuras, who were promised their portion of the divine drink. Mt Mandara was to be the churning rod, and serpent king Vasuki the rope. But they forgot about gravity . . . As soon as

they plonked the mountain in the ocean, well, it sank. And this was Vishnu's cue to enter the scene, as a turtle. Deep-diving to the ocean floor, he slid the sunken peak on his back and elevated it, holding it up all through the Samudra Manthan. Once the work was done, the amphibian became airborne, flew off with the mountain, put it back in place and disappeared.

#3 VARAHA THE BOAR

The next time Vishnu came down to aid the earth, literally, was when Bhumidevi, the earth goddess, was being tormented by the demon Hiranyaksha. This dude chased her all over the galaxy, so she finally jumped into the ocean and hid in a cave in the seabed. Vishnu received her telepathic message for help and appeared in the shape of a mammoth boar. So while the clueless demon was hunting for the earth, the helpful hog dived down into the depths, gently picked up the globe on his snout and carried her to safety. Once she was secure, he turned on Hiranyaksha. They fought an epic battle until the boar prevailed, using his sharp tusks and the divine mace, Kaumodaki. (Can you imagine how he used it?) Demon dead, order restored, time to go—and so, Vishnu set off back to peaceful Vaikuntha.

#4 NARASIMHA THE MAN-LION

Hiranyakashipu, asura brother of Hiranyaksha, had a boon from Brahma (who else), which made him pretty much invincible. He could not be killed by any weapon of metal, stone or steel; at night or day; indoors or outdoors; by man, god, asura, or beast; and on ground or in air! Twist in the tale: his son Prahlada was Vishnu's biggest fan. Despite Dad's no-no, this devotion continued. H tried to kill P, who escaped every time, so he decided to behead his son. Enter Narasimha in aid of his greatest devotee! A column at the palace threshold (neither indoors nor outdoors) split apart, a huge man-lion emerged (neither man, god, asura, nor beast), draped H over his thighs (neither on ground, nor in air) and tore him apart with his claws (no weapon). And what time was it? Dusk: neither day nor night. Devotee saved, asura dead and Narasimha merged with Vishnu.

#5 VAMANA, SHORT GUY WITH TALL PLANS

Powerful asura king Mahabali, grandson of Prahlada, was essentially a just ruler but intent on conquering all. Having subjugated the world of men, he turned upwards to attack Devaloka. Yet again, the devas lost—seems like they were not very good at defending their lands—and went crying for help to Brahma, who sent them to Vishnu. Obliging them again, the preserver turned into Vamana, a vertically challenged Brahmin, and toddled off to where Mahabali was conducting a sacrifice. V asked M for a boon; M was thrilled with his victory and promptly granted it. What was the boon? V would receive as much land as he could cover in three steps. *Ha*, thought M, *how far can this dwarf go? Ha*, thought V, and enlarged himself from gnome to giant in a jiffy. In this Trivikrama form, he took his strides, covering all of Earth in the first step, all of the heavens in the next, and then . . . nowhere to go! Realizing his folly, M offered his own head, where V placed his foot gently and pushed him down into the netherworld. (Basically, asuras—no matter how good or just—were not supposed to forget where they belonged!) However, pleased with M's adherence to Rajadharma (kingly duty), V promised him Indra's place in the next cycle of creation and allowed him to return to Earth once every year to be worshipped by his mortal (ex-)subjects, who had been quite happy to be ruled by M. This is celebrated as Onam every year.

Read more about this in 'Forever and a Day', page 64.

#6 PARASHURAMA, SAGE WITH A RAGE

The next avatar manifested the form of a chiranjeevi with an axe, Parashurama, son of sage Jamadagni. His aim was not to defeat asuras but to rid the world of the burden of Kshatriya arrogance. The first to meet his axe-blade was Kartavirya Arjuna, the thousand-armed Haihaya king. He was the world's most powerful king and acted the part, crushing anyone who opposed him. Provoked into a rage by the

Read more about this in 'Forever and a Day', page 59.

theft of his father's favourite cow, Surabhi (or Kamadhenu), Parashurama attacked the Haihaya army and killed the king. In revenge, the princes went and killed Jamadagni. That was it! Parashurama went berserk, attacking and

Read more about this in 'Forever and a Day', page 65.

wiping out one evil supercilious Kshatriya after another, until he had cleansed the land of the lot. This was the first time Vishnu didn't just appear but took birth as an avatar, and also the first time he didn't return to Vaikuntha after finishing his task.

#7 RAMA, KING WITH A CALLING

Vishnu's next human avatar was Rama, who came to rid the world of the evil perpetrated by Ravana, asura king of Lanka, and his cohorts. It appears that the entire scene was stage-managed such that Ravana kidnapped Sita (Rama's wife), causing a war in which he himself was finally killed. Many of his sons and his brother Kumbhakarna too died at the hands of Rama, his brother Lakshmana, *vanara* king Sugriva and Hanuman. In the Ramayana, two avatars came face to face (another first) and the torch of divinity was passed across when Parashurama handed over Vishnu's bow Sharanga to Rama, who had just broken Shiva's bow Pinaka in Sita's

Read more about this in 'Heavenly Hardware, Bulletproof Beings', page 186.

swayamvara. Once again, after fulfilling this mission, the avatar didn't immediately return to the heavens. He stayed on Earth to rule benevolently till it was time to retire. And then he walked into the river Sarayu to merge with Mahavishnu.

#8 KRISHNA, THE MIRACLE MAKER

The next avatar is a matter of debate. Some claim it was Krishna, the Yadava prince of Mathura, and others say it was actually his half-brother, Balarama. The reason why some do not count Krishna as *just* an avatar is that he has been the only 'incarnation' to display the mega 'Vishwaroop', containing all of creation within him. Indeed, Krishna showed divinity from even before his birth, which was foretold by an *akashvani*. In terms of the Dashavatar, he was born to kill the evil Shishupala and Dantavakra. He also came to provide humans with the truth of life, distilled into the Bhagavad Gita, which he recited to Arjuna as a sermon on the battlefield of Kurukshetra. Though human-born, Krishna performed superhuman feats, killing ferocious demons like Putana, Dhenukasura, Aghasura and Trinavarta, and holding up Govardhan on one finger for a whole week. He killed the famed wrestler Chanura and his own evil uncle Kamsa. He healed Trivakra the cripple, with just a touch. He could 'clone' himself so many times that each *gopi* who danced the *rasleela* had Krishna as her partner. He saved Yudhishthira from Durvasa's wrath by magically filling the stomachs of his retinue with just one grain of rice and one morsel of vegetable. He frustrated the Kauravas' evil and shameful plan, led by Dushasana, to disrobe their sister-in-law Draupadi, by making sure that her sari never ended. No matter how much they pulled, the garment wouldn't end and they

Read more about this in 'Thugs of Hindustan', page 233.

had to give up, exhausted. Of all the avatars, Krishna is easily the most divine yet the most human of all. We witness his boyish naughtiness as well as his cosmic power. Perhaps he was much more than a mere avatar.

#9 BUDDHA THE PACIFIST

 The end of Krishna's eventful stay on Earth led into Kali Yuga, which is indeed the age we live in. In this age, one avatar (though somewhat debatable) has appeared in the form of Gautama Buddha. Born as Siddhartha, son of Sakya king Shuddhodana, he renounced his worldly life to become an ascetic and, after a long time spent in austere meditation, he finally attained enlightenment under the Mahabodhi, a sacred peepul in Bodh Gaya. He then taught the world compassion, understanding and non-violence, hoping to make people look beyond the ritual and rigour of organized religion and actually find faith.

#10 KALKI THE HARBINGER

 If this epoch called Kali Yuga began with the end of Krishna's life on Earth, it is supposed to culminate with the arrival of the tenth and final incarnation of Vishnu: Kalki. Riding in on his white steed Devadatta, this cosmic judge will reward the good and just people, and blast out of existence those that demonstrate inhumanity or baseness. The world will end with pralaya, possibly a megaflood, and creation will begin all over again.

THE ZOROASTRIAN PANTHEON

VOHU MANO ('good mind') is one of the six amesha spentas, created by Ahura Mazda to fight him alongside in his constant conflict with the evil forces of Ahriman. According to tradition, the prophet Zoroaster was brought to Ahura Mazda by Vohu Mano, and everyone else who wishes to reach the Lord must approach him through this immortal. Of all the amesha spentas, he is the closest to Ahura Mazda. The second month of the Zoroastrian calendar is dedicated to him. His sacred animal is the cow, symbol of the goodness that provides nourishment.

ASHA VAHISHTA is perhaps the most popular amesha spenta, with more mentions compared to any other immortal in the Avestan Gathas (holy verse texts) composed by Zoroaster. With a name that indicates righteousness, purity and virtue, Asha Vahishta has the second day of the week and the second month of the year named for him. In ancient rituals, he used to be invoked with Atash, the spirit of fire. According to ancient Avestan stories, he is destined to come to Earth on the Day of Renovation, with the yazata Airyaman, and purge the land of all evil spirits.

VAIRYA, or **SHAHREWAR**, was unnamed in earlier Gathas but emerged as an amesha spenta in the Younger Avestan, a later collection of hymns. Earlier, the sky was thought to be of stone, but later this changed to crystal, considered both stone and metal. It was then that this immortal's domain became the world of metals,

and texts say that during the process of creation, Shahrewar took metal derived from the sky as his creation. He treats you well if you treat metal well, but torments you if you don't! Also, he sides with the underdog against bullies—hail Iron Man!

ARMAITI, the spirit of devotion or piety, guides humans to lead good lives towards salvation. As per Zoroaster, she has the closest relationship with Ahura Mazda, like a daughter, and he credits her with being his own guide to discovering truth. She is the divine protector of women, and her festival was a favoured time for courtship, the day when girls chose husbands for themselves. In worship rituals, Armaiti is represented by the sacred or holy space. Priests sit cross-legged on the floor, to be closer to the goddess who is said to be a form of the earth itself.

HAURVATAT (HORDAD) and **AMERETAT (AMURDAD)** are identified with water and plants (or wholeness) and Earth (or immortality), respectively. Hordad, the mildest of the amesha spentas, presides over the third calendar month, while Amurdad is the deity of the fifth. As protectors of plants, water and Earth, they undid Ahriman's evil when he made the primordial plant wither. They crushed the plant's remains and scattered them over Earth as rain, causing millions of plants to grow. Both, originally feminine, are sometimes considered masculine in later texts. However, Zoroaster's daughters are considered to be in the mould of this divine duo.

WHO AM I? _____

THE BUDDHIST PANTHEON

Buddhist tradition has stories not only of the Buddha but also of many Buddhas in the making, the bodhisattvas or enlightened beings who have put off attaining nirvana in order to help others attain it. Here are the eight bodhisattvas that are considered most important.

AKASHAGARBHA, 'womb or nucleus of space', is depicted as clad in pristine white robes, holding a lotus and a light sabre. (Of eastern wisdom, the light it emits, hmmm!) Known for his boundless generosity, he is likened to an affluent man who

derives immense satisfaction by distributing all his wealth to the needy. Owing to his association with the element of akasha or space, his knowledge and wisdom are said to be as boundless as space. He is sometimes known as the twin brother of the 'earth-womb' bodhisattva, Kshitigarbha.

KSHITIGARBHA, the other part of the womb pair, is a prominent figure in Mahayana Buddhism, worshipped as Dizang in China and Jizo in Japan. He is famed for vowing to not personally achieve Buddhahood until all hells are emptied. So, he is regarded as a saviour of lost souls. Depicted as a monk with a halo, he carries a staff to force open the gates of hell and a wish-fulfilling jewel to dispel darkness. The sutra of his great vows is said to have been spoken by the Buddha at the end of his life in homage to his mother, Mayadevi.

AVALOKITESHVARA, 'the lord who looks down', embodies the compassion of all the Buddhas and is called Padmapani, 'the lotus bearer'. Known (in female form) as Kuan Yin in China and Kannon in Japan, he is directly related to the mantra 'Om Mani Padme Hum'. As per the *Karandavyuha Sutra*, the sun and moon emerged from his eyes, Shiva from his brow, Brahma from his shoulders, Narayana from his heart, Saraswati from his teeth, the winds from his mouth, the earth from his feet and the sky from his stomach. Does this remind you of Krishna's Vishwaroop displayed in the court of Hastinapura?

MANJUSHRI or 'gentle glory' personifies supreme wisdom, even though he is shown holding an uplifted sword. One of the oldest bodhisattvas in the Mahayana tradition, he often plays the role

of the seeker, to whose questions the Buddha replies with his teachings and truths. His sword thus symbolizes the sharpness of wisdom. He is also shown holding the *Prajnaparamita Sutra* (Perfection of Wisdom). As the bodhisattva of intellectual excellence, the golden-hued Manjushri has featured in almost all Buddhist scriptures from sutras to commentaries to meditation manuals. Even today, Buddhist scholars seek his blessings at the beginning of their own works.

SAMANTABHADRA, 'universally worthy', forms the Shakyamuni trinity along with the Buddha and Manjushri. Representative of Buddhist practice and meditation, he is the patron of the *Lotus Sutra* and his ten great vows form the basis of Buddhahood. He is shown resting on a six-tusked white elephant, whose tusks symbolize the purity of the six senses. His great vows are to: 1. pay respect to all the Buddhas, 2. praise all the Buddhas, 3. make abundant offerings, 4. repent misdeeds and evil karma, 5. rejoice in others' merits, 6. request the Buddhas to continue teaching, 7. request the Buddhas to remain in the world, 8. always follow the teachings of the Buddhas, 9. accommodate and benefit all living beings and 10. transfer all merits and virtues to benefit all beings. The tenth vow is well practised with many Buddhists dedicating their merits and good works to all beings during Buddhist rituals.

VAJRAPANI, the most angry-looking of all bodhisattvas, gets his name from his weapon, the *vajra* or thunderbolt, which he is ready to hurl at any danger confronting the Buddha, whom he protects. Just as Avalokiteshvara represents the Buddha's compassion and Manjushri wisdom, Vajrapani symbolizes strength. Depicted as

standing in a warrior pose, he has the vajra in one hand and a lasso to bind demons (like Yama?) in the other. He wears a crown of skulls (shades of Kali?), has a third eye (Shiva, surely!), wears snakes around his neck like a garland and is clad in tiger skin (Shiva again).

SARVANIVARANA-VISHKAMBHIN, 'remover of hindrances' is invoked to ensure successful meditation by eliminating ignorance (*avijja*) and five associated obstacles that hinder the progress of cultivating the mind: 1. desire (*kamacchanda*), 2. ill will (*vyapada*), 3. sloth (*thina-middha*), 4. restlessness and regret (*uddhacca-kukkucca*) and 5. sceptical doubt (*vicikiccha*). He is depicted variously in art, at times blue, at others white. He may hold a sword (to cut away hindrances) and a book; he may make the *sparshamudra* (touching the earth) and a gesture of peace with his hands; or he may hold a lotus and a banner upon which is shown a sword.

MAITREYA is the eighth, and yet to appear, bodhisattva, waiting for the right time in Tushita heaven. His role is to preach yet again the teachings or the Dharma of Gautama Buddha, when men have completely forgotten the values of Buddhist philosophy. His name comes from Sanskrit for friendliness (*maitri*), and he is shown seated in European fashion on a throne. It is foretold that Maitreya will be born to Brahmins and will marry, but then renounce the world after his son's birth. He will meditate for seven days to attain Buddhahood and then spread Dharma globally yet again.

WHO ARE WE?

THE GLORIES OF TARA

The Buddhist saviour goddess Tara is the feminine counterpart of Avalokiteshvara. Manifesting in many forms, she is wisdom in action. Legend has it that a tear of A once fell to form a lake. From its waters emerged a lotus, which bloomed to reveal her inside. Like A, she is compassionate and helps men cross over from mortality to enlightenment. In iconography, Tara can appear in any colour, her hue symbolizing her temperament and role. Famously, she is Green Tara, who saves us from harm, and who is fearlessly wise. She can be White Tara, who bestows long life and healing, or Red Tara, who represents power, or Yellow Tara, who brings resources to the needy. Depicted in all colours and degrees of peacefulness and wrathfulness, with varying numbers of faces, arms and legs, this is one amazing goddess! There are likely close to 200 meditational forms of the enlightened Tara.

TUNES FOR TARA: *What songs would Tara have on her playlist, were she inclined musically? Here's your chance to play music director! Imagine Tara in different colours and moods, and pick songs for her. You can thematize the playlist by colour, mood, power or whatever you feel like. T(a)ra la la!*

3

SCENE UNSEEN

Legendary Places in Mythology

Being a land of countless myths, India is home to innumerable legendary places where these myths played out, such as the battlefield in Mahabharata or Patala, the multilevel parking for lost souls. India is also a land where, through its multiple myths, people believe in fantastic places found all over the cosmos, such as the super tall Mount Qaf that holds up the earth or the Chinvat Peretu that shifts shape based on the purity of the soul crossing over.

I f we like to believe that the stories found in world myths actually happened and that the people in these stories existed, well then, let us also believe that it all happened . . . somewhere. But where? Mythologies abound with places of magic, some bursting with happiness and goodness, others heavy with grief and terror. There are abodes of gods and anti-gods, including lofty mountains and unfathomably deep oceans. Forests crawl with beasts and sprites, cities float on timeless clouds. Let's take a walk through some of these legendary lands.

VAIKUNTHA, AN IDEAL LAND

Vaikuntha is the home of Vishnu, who preserves the cosmic order. He lives there with his consort, Shri or Lakshmi, the goddess of fortune. They recline on Ananta or Sheshanaga, the divine serpent whose many hoods cover them like umbrellas. Vishnu, who is part of the powerful triumvirate, is attended by Jaya and Vijaya, his doorkeepers and other assistants, of which there are countless. For it is in Vaikuntha that Vishnu is also manifested in thousands of forms, each with its own followers, friends, attendants, relatives, devotees—and each form indulging in a different activity!

Now, Vaikuntha is not on this plane of the human world. It is said to begin 26 million yojanas above Brahmaloka, the highest place in the material world. As per the *Vishnu Purana*, one yojana equals 12 km, so Vaikuntha is pretty far, far away. There is nothing above and beyond it, and it is also forever. *Say what?* Let's try to

place it in a physical, topographical context. If we map it out according to Puranic traditions and methods of astrogeography, Vaikuntha lies in the constellation of Capricorn.

According to traditional texts, Vaikuntha is full of gardens with wish-fulfilling trees (isn't that amazing?), beings that have no form or shape but are full of light, fountains of crystal-clear water and creepers whose flowers drip honey! Nothing goes wrong there; everything is good and just and right. Beings that reach Vaikuntha have escaped the Karmic cycle of births. They have no greed, no anger, no hatred, no material passions, no fear. They are in a state of nirvana.

BRAHMALOKA, A PERFECT LAND

Just like Vishnu, Brahma, the Creator of the cosmos, has his own world. According to some legends, Brahma sits on a lotus that grows out from, well, Vishnu's navel! Others say that his world is the highest in the plane of existence that is accessible to mortals. In Brahmaloka, he lives with Saraswati, the goddess of knowledge, and Gayatri, the personification of the mantra of the same name. Do you know the Gayatri Mantra?

This land is also called Satyaloka, or 'abode of truth'. Quite like Vaikuntha, it is believed to be a garden filled with beautiful and fragrant flowers and is sited on top of Mount Meru, the highest mountain in the known world.

GAYATRI MANTRA

The Gayatri Mantra, a hymn to the sun god, first appeared in the Rig Veda and is mentioned in the Upanishads as well as the Bhagavad Gita. Chanting it three times a day with complete focus is said to help our mental and spiritual growth. Here is the mantra in Sanskrit with a transliteration and a translation in English.

ॐ भूर्भुवः स्वः

Om Bhurbhuvah Svaha

तत्सवितुर्वरेण्यं

Tatsaviturvarenyam

भर्गो देवस्य धीमहि

Bhargo Devasya Dhimahi

धियो यो नः प्रचोदयात्

Dhiyo Yo Nah Prachodayat

'The eternal, the earth, the air, the heaven
That glory, that resplendence of the sun
May we meditate on its brilliance
May the sun inspire our minds'

In Buddhist tradition, Brahmaloka consists of a whopping twenty heavens: nine ordinary Brahma-worlds, five *suddhavasa* (pure abode), four *arupa* (formless), one *asannasatta* (consciousnessless) and one *vehapphala,* the highest, the purest. The inhabitants of all these heavens, except for the arupa worlds, are corporeal, which means they have a definite form and shape. But there are no females in this *loka* . . . wonder why?

You can be born in Brahmaloka if you live a life of complete virtue and also meditate a lot. Buddhists believe that when a kappa or kalpa ends—when the worlds are destroyed—then all the inhabitants of Brahmaloka will descend to spread humanity across creation once again.

SHAMBHALA, A SECRET LAND

Staying with the mythology of Buddhism, let's travel to the legendary land of Shambhala. They say it was a secret kingdom in not just Tibetan but also Chinese (who called it Hsi Tien), Hindu (Aryavarta, by some accounts) and Russian (Belovoyde) myths. It has been called by over a thousand names—Forbidden Land, Land of White Waters, Land of Radiant Spirits, Land of the Living Fire, Land of the Living Gods, Land of Wonders to name a few. It actually predates Buddhism in the Tibetan region where it was said to be located.

But where is it exactly? No one knows! Since ancient times, explorers have hunted high and low for this mythical paradise, but none has found it. Ancient Tibetan texts locate it in Punjab or Himachal Pradesh in India. Mongol legends place it in Siberia, where local folklore reinforces it by saying that Mount Belukha is the gateway to Shambhala. Incidentally, from as far away as South America comes a connected legend. There is a place named Apu Putucusi, right next to the mysterious Incan citadel of Machu Picchu in Peru. According to local legend, it is the entrance to a crystal city of light, the Incan

counterpart of Shambhala. Most modern Buddhist accounts place it in Tibet, where the Shambhala guardians protect its ultra-secret location.

Shambhala's exact position, both in geography and in scripture, may be unclear, but it is clear that the earliest text that refers to it in detail is the Kalachakra sutra. Interestingly, this text was composed, or pronounced, by the Buddha himself at the request of the King of Shambhala! According to it, Shambhala is yet to be reached when the forces of evil completely take over the world, the mists will lift to reveal this magical space and its

ruler will defeat the evil. Here, one catches echoes of a Hindu legend too. According to the *Vishnu Purana*, Kalki—the tenth and final avatar of Vishnu—will be born there and he will bring an end to the world drowning in evil so that good may resurface and restart.

His Holiness the Fourteenth Dalai Lama asserts that Shambhala is a place that is not physical; it is inside our minds, our souls. Inside us, there is a constant fight between evil and good, so it is up to us to ensure that good wins over evil. This resonates with the belief some people hold that Shambhala is a land where only pure hearts can exist, where love rules and where people do not suffer or grow old.

Can such a place indeed exist? There could be a simple explanation to why no one has found it yet. Many people are convinced that Shambhala is located at the end of the physical world because it is a bridge that connects this world to what lies beyond.

CHINVAT PERETU, A LAND OF JUDGEMENT

Speaking of bridges, in Zoroastrianism (or the Avestan tradition), there is mention of a Bridge of the Requiter, called Chinvat Peretu. It is mentioned in the Gathas, which are hymns believed to have been composed by Zoroaster or Zarathustra himself. Variously called Bridge of Separation and Bridge of Judgement, it is said to lie atop the peak of the cosmic mountain Harburz, with one end leading up to paradise and the other down to hell.

All souls that pass on have to cross this bridge, but the bridge changes it shape and size depending on the soul that is about to cross! Guarded by the deities of Sraosha ('conscience'), Mithra ('covenant') and Rashnu ('justice'), Chinvat Peretu acts like a filter. If the dead person performed more good deeds than misdeeds, the bridge widens and allows its soul to pass through quite easily. If not, it becomes narrower and narrower, forcing the soul to fall into the hands of the demon Vizaresh and reach hell.

PATALA, A LAND OF LOWS

Speaking of hell, there are multiple hells in most mythologies. In Hindu tradition, the universe is divided into three regions: Swarga or heaven for the gods; Mrityuloka or Earth for us humans; and Patala or hell for asuras, rakshasas and other demonic beings. It is also the home of the nagas, who were banished there by Brahma when they became too many to live on the earth's surface. Now this hell or the netherworld has seven levels: Atala, Vitala, Sutala, Rasatala, Talatala, Mahatala, and finally, Patala, the lowest. These levels, as well as the earth that is 70,000 yojanas higher, are supported on the head of the thousand-headed Sheshanaga. And below Patala lies Naraka, the place of death, where sinners are punished.

Hindu myth refers to the nagas as guardians of treasure. (Reminds you of Smaug, doesn't it?) Patala is full of palaces decorated with precious gems and fringed by lush groves. Many of these have been designed and built by Maya, the asura counterpart of Vishwakarma. In fact, some Puranic sources (including an

apparent account of the netherworlds by Narada) say that Patala is more beautiful and wonder-filled than even Swarga! There may be no sunlight that far below, but there is no darkness either. Resplendent jewels worn by the residents reflect enough to light up the entire place. Also, there is no old age or disease, not even sweat! Its inhabitants are happy and live not just in comfort but indeed in luxury. The air holds a sweet fragrance and a sweet music. The soil is multihued: white, black, purple, brown, yellow, gold. The supreme ruler of Patala is Bali, grandson of Prahlada, since Vishnu (as Vamana) pushed him into the netherworld. Individually, the seven different levels have their own rulers.

Buddhism too includes a concept of Patala as a multilevelled world beneath the earth. It is populated by asuras and nagas. In fact, Patala was established after the defeat of the asuras by Shakra (another name for Indra), who invoked Manjushri, the Boddhisattva of wisdom, for this purpose. The Vajrayana Buddhists believe that Patala can be entered through caves where asuras live. In many tales, these asuras—especially the females—are converted to Buddhism by well-known figures such as Padmasambhava.

AMARAVATI, A LAND OF LORDS

Up above the sky so high, high above all Patalas is Swarga, home of the devas in Hindu tradition. Its capital Amaravati is the city of Indra, more than 1000 km in circumference and bursting with Nandan Udyan, pleasure gardens with endless supplies

of fruit and flowers. It is said that its *sabhagar* (meeting hall) could fit in 350 million celestials as well as 48,000 rishis *and* a multitude of attendants! Some sources located it on the slopes of Mount Meru.

MOUNT MERU, A LAND HIGH ABOVE

Also called Sumeru or Mahameru, Meru is a five-peaked, uber-lofty mountain sacred to Hindus, Jains as well as Buddhists. The highest mountain in existence, it sits at the centre of the physical, the metaphysical and the spiritual worlds.

Some texts say that Meru Parvat lies exactly in the middle of the earth, in Jambudwipa. Others suggest that it is in the middle of the earth but unseen. And some believe that it lies north of Mount Kailash, so somewhere north of India. As per the Matsya and Bhagavata Puranas, it is 84,000 yojanas tall. It extends down into the nether regions as far as it extends up into the heavens. It rises up to Swarga and the Pole Star (Dhruva Tara) shines directly above it. The sacred river Ganga descends from Swarga on to its slopes, purifying the entire mountain in all four directions. It is the home of gods, and its foothills are the Himalayas. Most major deities have their kingdoms on or near it; their devotees reside with them on Meru, waiting for reincarnations.

Tibetan Buddhists believe that Meru is home to Demchok, an angry spirit somewhat akin to Shiva in his Rudra form. Jains hold the belief that there are two sets of a sun and a moon that revolve around Meru, turn by turn.

Mount Meru has inspired numerous temples, which use it as a model for the shikhara, or roof tower crowning the shrine. For instance, in Angkor Wat—the world's largest religious monument—five stone towers symbolize the five peaks of Meru. Indeed, this design is common to Hindu and Jain temples as well as Buddhist pagodas.

KAILASH, A LAND OF SNOWS AND MYSTERIES

Somehow all legendary places are very far away, right? Well, deep in the Himalayas of Tibet lies its crown, the majestic Mount Kailash. It is the only divine abode that has a physical form on Earth. The mountain is sacred to many religions. For the Hindus, it is the home of Shiva, his family, and his ganas. For the Buddhists, who call it Kangri (or Gangs) Rinpoche ('precious snow mountain'), it is the navel of the universe. For followers of Tibet's older Bon religion, it is the *axis mundi*, the centre of the world, the 'nine-storey swastika mountain'. For Hindus as well as Buddhists, Mount Kailash is the physical form of Mount Meru.

Late in the twentieth century, a team of Russian geologists, historians and physicists undertook an expedition to Kailash and concluded that it is actually a gargantuan pyramid that was built by men in ancient times. It is surrounded by many smaller pyramids and is a hub of paranormal activities. An urban legend, perhaps?

Well, a local legend tells the tale of the conflict between Milarepa, the champion of Vajrayana Buddhism, and Naro Bonchung, the Bon hero. The two battled for days and days, and since both were equally matched, neither gained the upper hand. Finally, it was decided that the one who reached the summit of Kailash first would be declared the winner of the divine duel. Promptly, Naro sat astride his magic drum and flew off towards the peak. Meanwhile, Milarepa straightened his spine, aligned his thoughts and meditated. And meditated . . . And meditated.

Then, just when it seemed that he would be left sitting at the post, he arose and climbed a ray of sunlight; he was instantly transported to the top of the mountain. Victory for Buddhism! Signal for the Bon religion to slide down and fade out. (So, that would also make Milarepa the only human—yes, he was a revered eleventh-century poet-saint—to have scaled Kailash!)

Jain mythology also venerates the peak because it is believed that their first *tirthankara*, Rishabhadeva or Adinatha, gained nirvana on this peak.

Near Kailash are two lakes, almost like the yin and yang of water bodies. There is the famed Mansarovar, a dip in which is believed to rid the soul of all its sins, of all times. It is believed that Shiva and Parvati and their ganas and apsaras, all of who still live atop the mountain, descend to bathe in the lake in the auspicious hour of Brahma-Muhurta, which is about an hour and a half before sunrise. *Brrrr!*

The opposite of this spiritual space is Rakshas Tal, the other lake believed to have been created when the demon king Ravana performed intense penance to please Shiva. It is said that because of its association with the great demon, Rakshas Tal has super salty water and does not have any aquatic life, neither fauna nor flora.

Once, Ravana even tried to lift Kailash to prove his strength. Not to be outdone, Shiva pressed it down with his little toe and crushed Ravana's hands. Trapped and immobile, Ravana then sang in praise of Shiva. He was quite a good musician and managed to impress the angry god, who not only released him but also gifted him the famed sword Chandrahasa.

In a way, Kailash is the opposite of the timeless land of Shambhala where people just don't age. In Kailash, there is such a high level of mystic energy that humans age super-swiftly. Pilgrims and travellers have shared tales of their hair and nails growing at a much faster rate than usual.

MOUNT QAF, A LAND OF CHALLENGES

Staying with mythical mountains, let's move to Islam. Though it is not renowned for its 'mythology', Islam has legendary places in its traditions. One such is Mount Qaf, a mysterious peak regarded as the 'farthest point of the earth', owing to its location at the far side of the ocean encircling the earth. It is huge! As big and tall as all the other mountains in the world. It is also considered to be the only place where the roc (or *simurgh,* in Persian legend), the giant bird, will land. Hmm, seems similar to Mount Meru?

Read more about this in 'Fantastic Beasts and Here You Find Them', page 117.

According to Islamic legend, Allah created the world flat, held in place by 'pegs' of mountains all around its edge. It rests on the back of a giant bull that stands on a gigantic fish in a bowl supported by an angel. Some interpretations say that Mount Qaf is the central peak of all these mountains, while others say that it is indeed the entire chain. Like most mythical challenges, it cannot be easily crossed by men. It is loaded with traps and deserts, djinns and spirits.

At a spiritual and symbolic level, one can interpret the legend thus: Mount Qaf represents the struggle of man and mankind, the peak or peaks being the physical and metaphysical challenges

and obstacles and trials that life brings. If one can scale the mountain and somehow reach its summit, it would be similar to finding one's true self and becoming one with God!

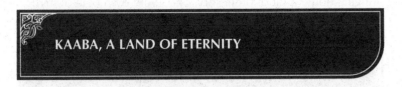

KAABA, A LAND OF ETERNITY

The holiest of the holy for Muslims, the Kaaba is another one of those places of legend that also actually exist. Located in the city of Mecca in Saudi Arabia, it is the site of a shrine that was built originally by Adam, and then rebuilt by Ibrahim (Abraham) and his son Ismail (Ishmael) after it was destroyed by the Great Flood of the time of Nuh (Noah).

It is known as the 'house of God' (*Bayt Allah*), and is cuboid in shape—perhaps the world's most recognizable cuboid. (If it were a cube, it would possibly compete for that title with Rubik's cube!) At its eastern corner is a black stone, which is said to have been given to Prophet Muhammad ﷺ to set into the walls. Every year, millions of pilgrims make the journey called haj (or umrah, if it is not within the specified time period), to pray at this holy place.

Imagine this dramatic scene: a jaw-dropping 6 million pilgrims gathered at the same time in the same space, together doing the tawaf, circumambulations performed by going around the Kaaba seven times counterclockwise, the first three times quickly and nearer the edge of the courtyard, and the last four times slower, nearer the Kaaba . . . Almost hypnotic, no?

Another legend-turned-real place found here is Zamzam Well, the fountain of water that sprang out of the desert to save the lives of Ismail (Ishmael) and his mother Hajar (Hagar), the wife of Ibrahim. The water from this fountain is considered holy, and is taken back by all hajis for their relatives and families. It's like bringing home a bit of prehistory, one's very own byte of myth.

A MAP OF MYTHS

Now that you have read about the fascinating places in various mythologies, let's see how good your mytho-geography has become! Can you solve the clues and fill up this acrostic? Once you've filled in all the letters for clues 1 to 10, #11 will emerge, like magic! It will be something you have already read about in this section.

CLUES

1. Fabled mountain sacred to Shiva
2. Literally 'world worker'; the divine architect
3. Highly aspirational place, where Vishnu lives
4. Capital city of the devas, its name meant 'the place of the deathless ones'
5. What the Tibetans call the answer to clue #1
6. Abode of Brahma, 'the place of truth'
7. Lowest of the nether regions, which gives them their collective name
8. Tibetan Bon priest who fought long and hard with Milarepa in a decisive battle that left Buddhism as the main religion of the region
9. Saline lake near Kailash, said to be the spiritual opposite of Mansarovar
10. Demon who lies in wait for souls beneath the legendary bridge, Chinvat Peretu

LIVING LEGENDS

We may not be in the era of legend any more, but some of its symbols live on. Let's check out some places in India where the line between what's real and what's myth get blurred. We give you the clues, and you need to work out the answers by jogging your memory or opening some search tabs on your laptop.

1. This small town in Parvati Valley is where Parvati lost an earring, Shiva flew into a rage and Sheshanaga hissed to boil the waters of the Beas so that it would throw up more gems . . . and that is why it still has hot springs! Can you name the town?

2. Anjaneyadri or Anjaneya Hill in Hampi (Karnataka), atop which sits a temple where the Ramayana is recited in Sanskrit and not Kannada, and is believed to be the birthplace of a mighty hero of legend. Who is it? _____

3. On his mission to bring back the Sanjeevani Booti to revive Lakshmana from his coma, the personage in clue #2 got confused among the thousands of herbs on this mountain in the Valley of Flowers, so he uprooted the entire mountain and flew back with it! Which mountain is it? _____

4. This hill station of Madhya Pradesh is home to many caves— caves where the Pandavas took shelter during their exile in the Mahabharata, caves where ancient Buddhist monks meditated and caves where Shiva hid from Bhasmasura, who could turn anything he touched to ash. What place is this?
    _____

5. There is a growing belief that Jesus survived the Crucifixion and went away from Golgotha to live in Kashmir in India. This shrine in Srinagar is believed to contain the tomb of Jesus of Nazareth. Can you name it? _____

4

FOREVER AND A DAY

The Immortals in Mythology

Gods live forever. Anyone born to mortals, however, must exit the world some day. That day has not yet arrived for the Chiranjeevis, 'those who live permanently'. And in this chapter, we talk about this concept of immortality and beings who, legend has it, live forever!

'Ask me for anything. Any one thing, and you shall have it.' Imagine that a powerful being grants you such a boon.

To this, you might say: 'My one wish is that all my wishes should come true, now and for ever.'

Well, it usually isn't that simple because there is always some disclaimer or other! It's like in the myths: a demon craves immortality, overcomes the severest of challenges over thousands of years to please whichever deity can grant him the boon and finally gets the boon, but there is always a catch, a condition.

Remember King Hiranyakashipu, who had Brahma's blessing that he couldn't be killed by any human or animal, neither inside nor outside, neither in the day nor at night? Well, it seemed like he tried to cover all his bases, but the thing is there's always a loophole. In this case, Vishnu took on his Narasimha avatar (half-man and half-lion), lurked inside a pillar till dusk (the twilight time between day and night) and then killed Hiranyakashipu at the palace threshold (neither inside nor really outside).

Terms and conditions may apply for asuras, but there are, in fact, a few 'immortals' in Hindu mythology. These are the Chiranjeevis, a term that combines the Sanskrit words for 'eternal' (*chiram*) and 'living' (*jeevi*). Traditionally, there are seven: Ashwatthama, the accursed son of Drona; asura king Bali, who was pressed into the underworld by Vishnu in his Vamana form; Veda Vyasa, who composed the Mahabharata; Hanuman, the mindful monkey; Vibhishana, who was apparently granted immortality by Brahma (but only for one cycle of yugas); Kripa, guru to the Kauravas and the Pandavas; and Parashurama, the former avatar of Vishnu.

अश्वत्थामा बलिर्व्यासो हनुमांश्च विभीषणः
कृपश्च परशुरामम सप्तैते चिरंजीवनम
सप्तैतान् संस्मरेन्नित्यं मार्कण्डेयमथाष्टमम्
जीवेद्वर्षशतं सोपि सर्वव्याधिविवर्जितः

The Chiranjeevi shloka translates as: 'Ashwatthama, Bali, Vyasa, Hanuman, Vibhishana, Kripa and Parashurama are the seven Chiranjeevis, the death-defeating or evergreen beings. By remembering their names along with Markandeya, the eighth, a man gains freedom from sickness and disease and can live up to a hundred years.' The eighth name on the list is Markandeya, the sage who was destined to die when he was sixteen years old but defied death and Yama, Lord of Death, through his resolute belief in Shiva and by hanging on to a Shiva lingam for dear life!

With the passage of time, more entities have been added to this list: Jambavan, the king of bears who allied with Rama against Ravana; Kag Bhushundi, a sage living in the form of a crow; Muchkunda, the king-turned-sage whose sleep you shouldn't disrupt or you might be *bhasmo*-ed (and that would hurt!); the timeless tortoise Akupara on whose carapace stand four elephants who, in turn, hold up the earth; the serpent Sheshanaga, whose other name is Ananta or 'eternal'; and the group of saptarishis, the evolved beings who manifest themselves in every manvantara to help the world deal with pralaya.

GRIN AND BEAR IT

We know Jambavan as the king of bears, who was loyal to Rama and helped him fight Ravana. What we don't know is that this beastly bhagwan also had incredible strength, wisdom and leadership skills. And that he also appeared in the Mahabharata, where he wrestled with Krishna over Syamantaka, the resplendent gem that gave Surya his dazzle, but was stolen. Some people theorize that the gem is actually the Koh-i-noor diamond!

TIMELESS TREE

It appears that 'Chiranjeev-ism' is not limited only to animated beings like men, asuras and apemen. The Akshaya Vat (literally 'the indestructible tree') is said to be an immortal, or Chiranjeevi, tree. One legend has it that when the sage Markandeya asked Lord Vishnu to show him a sign of power, the latter flooded the entire world (only for an instant, though), and the only living object visible above the floodwaters was the Akshaya Vat, the banyan tree that obviously didn't give a fig . . . Literally! You may ask, where is this miraculous plant? There are quite a few that lay claim to the fame. One is in Patalpuri in Allahabad (now Prayagraj), where Rama, Sita and Lakshmana are said to have rested, and the Jain tirthankara Rishabhadeva is said to have meditated. Another claimant stands in Gaya, and yet another in Varanasi. Buddhists believe that the Bodhi Tree in Gaya is a manifestation of Akshaya Vat. Er, but since the existing Bodhi Tree is an offshoot of an older offshoot of the original one (taken to Sri Lanka by Mahendra, son of Ashoka), this is likely not the real deal. Tibetans believe that the Buddha planted a seed from the original on the slopes of Mount Kailash. It would certainly need divine blessings to have survived there!

Can you imagine living for *that* long? An eternal existence may be a blessing for some, a burden for others. Let's take a look at these timeless legends to find out.

BALI, THIRD TIME LUCKY

Bali, the grandson of Prahlada, was a great asura king, so powerful that he was also known as 'Mahabali'. Having conquered this world as well as the netherworld, he set his sights on the divine world, Devaloka. As usual, Indra and his posse couldn't withstand the mighty asura armies for long and made a run for it, straight to Vishnu to help them reclaim their space. And as usual, he obliged.

While Bali was performing the Ashwamedha horse sacrifice, Vishnu assumed the form of the dwarf Vamana and asked the king for alms. Feeling all-powerful and mega generous, Bali asked Vamana to name his desire. Vamana asked for land, as much land as he could cover in three paces. *Uh, what?* Bali probably sniggered inwardly, as he agreed despite warnings from his street-smart guru, who suspected some trickery. In a flash, Vamana grew to a gigantic size and took his paces. With his first, he covered Patala and Prithvi. With his second, the heavens. Bali realized in dismay that he owned no more land, and Vamana was yet to take the third step! He bowed and asked Vamana to place his foot on his head. Well, here was Vamana/Vishnu's chance . . . He pressed Bali down, straight into Patala. (He didn't harm him, though, because his grandfather Prahlada appeared and asked Vishnu to spare Bali's life.)

Since Bali had followed rajadharma even in a challenging situation, Vishnu made him the lord of the netherworld, who would live forever and be allowed to return once every year to

Prithvi to meet his subjects. This visit is celebrated in Kerala as Onam. In fact, Vishnu also declared that Bali would be the Indra of the next manvantara and rule the heavens.

PARASHURAMA, THE SAGE WITH THE RAGE

'Rama of the Axe' or Parashurama, the fiery-tempered son of Jamadagni and Renuka, was one of the avatars of Vishnu. He was born to knock the stuffing out of the puffed-up Kshatriyas, who had forgotten their dharma and were traumatizing common folk instead of protecting them. Without beating about the bush, Parashurama went straight for Kartavirya Arjuna, the king of the Haihayas, and the most powerful of all kings of the time.

The plot unfolded when the 'thousand-armed' Kartavirya Arjuna came to Jamadagni's ashram and forcibly took away the holy cow named Surabhi. And so, Parashurama went after him and got the cow back after chopping off all thousand arms of the king, killing him and defeating his men. *Ouch!* Swearing revenge, the princes attacked the hermitage and killed Jamadagni, at a time when Parashurama was not at the ashram. On his return, he decided that the time had come for all conceited and power-mad Kshatriyas to be taught a lesson. Armed with his axe Vidyudabhi, which he had received from Shiva after extreme penance, he went after the wayward warriors, wiping out generations of Kshatriyas over and over again twenty-one times, until his ancestor Richika, one of the saptarishis, urged him to stop. When his anger subsided and he realized that his mission as an avatar

had been accomplished, Parashurama headed to the mountains (Mahendragiri) and became a hermit.

Mythologist Devdutt Pattanaik has an interesting take on this. He suggests that Parashurama is immortal to defend the earth as he killed all the warriors himself. Touché!

The hot-headed hermit had other roles to play too, in later legends. He was the one who challenged Rama to string Vishnu's bow (which he carried) after hearing that Rama had broken Shiva's bow in Sita's swayamvara. In the Mahabharata, he tutored Bhishma, Drona and Karna in the skills of war. It is believed that he still lives somewhere in the mountains. If you are near Mahendragiri in Odisha, you may just catch sight of this venerable old man!

WHOSE WAR IS IT?

Given that there were so many wars in legend, there were also so many warriors, and so many levels of warriors, based on their warfare skills and mastery of weapons. The highest level is known as Mahamaharathi, and only two beings achieved this label: Shiva and Kali, who could both finish off the entire universe in the blink of an eye. The next level, and effectively the most formidable one, is Atimaharathi, which is a warrior equal to twelve Maharathis. Parashurama, along with Krishna, Hanuman and Indrajit, is considered one of the very few Atimaharathi warriors born on Earth.

Read more about this in 'Call of Deity: Legendary Warfare', page 175.

HANUMAN, THE ORIGINAL SUPERHERO

The most loved and worshipped deity in India must be Hanuman. He is your friend, the one you pray to for things big and small. He is the icon of loyalty. Rama's most devout follower, he is said to have ripped open his chest to show how Rama and Sita were literally stamped on his heart. (Bet he too had Wolverine-like healing abilities!)

Born to Kesari and Anjana, Hanuman was a precocious baby. Some say he was a creation of the blessings of Shiva, some call him Vayuputra, while others say that Anjana partook of the prasad from Dasharatha's *putrakameshti yagna* (a ceremony to ask the gods to bless him with a son), which yielded Rama. Whatever his origin, he was superstrong and super brave. As a child, he once flew right up to the sun, to gobble it, thinking it was a giant mango! It took Indra's vajra to knock him down to Earth! Later stories of his strength and determination are even more fascinating. He could change his size at will, dash across huge distances at hyper-speed, pick up and fly with entire mountain peaks, defeat monsters with his wit and smarts, and save his lord from certain death, even going into the underworld to defeat just about everyone and rescue Rama and Lakshmana.

Brahma made Hanuman almost invincible; no one could kill him with any weapon in any war. He was blessed with the power of creating fear in his enemies but destroying fear in his friends. He could assume any form, travel anywhere. Shiva gave him a long, long life with the ability to cross the ocean, wisdom

of the scriptures and a band that would protect him for life. Varuna blessed him with immunity from water. Agni protected him from burning. Surya gave him the blessings of yoga *laghima* and *garima*, so he could shrink and expand at will. Yama blessed him with good health and immunity from weapons. Kubera gave him eternal happiness and satisfaction. Vayu gave him the speed of the wind.

It is believed that when Rama was leaving the earth, he asked Hanuman to come along. In response, Hanuman asked permission to stay on Earth for as long as the people of the earth chanted the name of Rama in devotion. Well, that's why he is said to still exist on this planet!

So how was it that Hanuman became Sugriva's minister? Apparently, he wanted to learn about the world and went to Surya, who could see all that happened. As *guru dakshina*, Surya asked Hanuman to help his son, Sugriva. So now you know.

TULSI'S TIME WARP

Goswami Tulsidas, the poet-saint who wrote *Ramcharitmanas*, apparently 'met' Hanuman a few times. In the sixteenth century, that too! What's more, he prayed to the eternal simian to arrange a darshan of Rama. Hanuman obliged him and Tulsi managed to see Rama on the Ganga's ghats in Varanasi. In fact, legend has it that Rama even put a sandalwood tilak on Tulsi, because the latter was so ecstatic at the sight of his lord that he just couldn't move. Could an episode like this have taken place? Do the divine really walk among us? What can explain this experience of Tulsidas?

VIBHISHANA, FACED WITH A TOUGH CHOICE

The youngest son of sage Vishravas and Kaikesi, the younger brother of Ravana and Kumbhakarna, Vibhishana was 'pure of heart and deed'. Although he was an asura, he lived his life to a high standard of dharma, pious in thought and action. When the three brothers prayed to Brahma, all seeking immortality, he was indeed the only one who received it. (The gods do demonstrate some foresight, huh?)

When he advised his (more famous or infamous) brother Ravana to return Sita to Rama, his popularity ranking in Lanka took a massive skydive. So, he took his mother's advice to leave the kingdom and decided to serve Rama. Vibhishana's conscience was very clear on this issue of fighting against (what has gone down in legend as 'betraying') his brother and fellow rakshasas. He was with the side that he believed was good and just, and against the side that he believed was in the wrong. In fact, his advice to Rama proved invaluable and led directly to the defeat and deaths of, first, Meghnad, and finally, Ravana.

After the war, when leaving for Ayodhya, Rama crowned Vibhishana the king of Lanka and entrusted him with the duty of staying on Earth to guide people on the path of dharma.

VED VYASA, THE KEEPER OF LEGENDS

Originally named Krishna Dwaipaayana (named so because he was dark-skinned and born on an island), Vyasa is ranked as one of the greatest sages of Indian legend. People believe that he is still alive and living among us, or somewhere in the Himalayas, till the end of this Kali Yuga.

He is the creator of the Mahabharata, and is said to have composed and recited the verses of the epic so fast that Ganesha, who was writing it down, could barely keep up. *Epic rapping!* In a way, Vyasa was retelling the story of his own family, being the son of Satyavati, who was the wife of the emperor Shantanu and the great-grandmother of the Pandavas as well as the Kauravas. His father was the sage Parashara, also a great scholar of the scriptures. Vyasa himself was the father of Dhritarashtra, Pandu, Vidura and Suka.

Having seen the adventures of four generations of the Kuru race made Vyasa the perfect choice to document their tale, one that ended with the greatest battle ever seen, the Kurukshetra war. His mind was bursting with the story in verse form, and he needed someone to write the whole thing down as he spoke, or else he wouldn't be able to compose it properly. Ganesha was his first and only choice for scribe, because he was astute and wrote really well too. Now, the elephant-headed god had his own condition: he would do the job only if Vyasa narrated the entire tale without a pause; if he paused, Ganesha would quit. Vyasa countered with one of his own: that Ganesha wouldn't write any

verse down unless he understood it perfectly. This barter gave Vyasa, on and off, some time to pause, collect his thoughts, and even take a breath . . . And this is how the greatest tale ever told came to be written.

KRIPACHARYA, THE TIMELESS TEACHER

He is one of the characters you may not have heard much about, one of those who almost slip under the radar. But we are not going to let him! Kripacharya, whom you will meet again later, was the guru of the Kaurava and Pandava princes of Hastinapura. Respected for his impartiality, he gave them lessons from

Read more about him in 'Binary Beings', page 100.

the scriptures, tutored them on how to use assorted, amazing weapons and groomed them so they could be good princes and kings. Like any good teacher, when he felt that they needed a better instructor for the finer art of war, he handed them over to his brother-in-law Dronacharya, who was himself a disciple of Parashurama.

To show his gratitude to the Kauravas for nurturing him with food and shelter, Kripacharya fought in their faction in the great war of Kurukshetra. He did so even though he knew that the Kauravas used wrong, immoral methods to try to win. He was particular about following the principles of dharma, but he was also loyal and impartial. He did not judge the Kauravas; in fact, he helped Ashwatthama in the midnight slaughter of the Pandava camp after the war, which was completely against all

codes of combat. Owing to his strength of character—marked by unshakeable loyalty, impartiality and integrity in the face of the greatest challenges—he was granted a boon of immortality by Krishna.

Kripacharya was a magnificent warrior. Bhishma described him as a Maharathi, who could single-handedly fight off 60,000 soldiers. Let's take at least sixty seconds to process that and think of him as part of the Avengers ensemble! He was also one of only three survivors on the losing side. Later on, he found himself back in favour with Hastinapura's new rulers. Legend has it that when the Pandavas crowned Parikshit, Arjuna's grandson, king and left on their journey to the Himalayas, they appointed Kripacharya as his guru.

ASHWATTHAMA, NOT EXACTLY A GEM OF A GUY

You've already read about Dronacharya and Kripacharya, gurus to the Kaurava and Pandava princes. Well, the former was Ashwatthama's father and the latter, his uncle. Instructed in the art of war by these two amazing tutors, he was easily one of the best warriors of his age.

He was also born with a gem embedded in his forehead. (Remember Vision and his Mind Stone?) This gave him power over all living beings lower than humans and protected him from hunger, thirst and fatigue.

Because he was friends with Duryodhana, Ashwatthama fought for the Kauravas in the Kurukshetra war. He was the last commander of the Kaurava army, which numbered only three at

the end. Yes, that's how intense the battle was. The night after the battle, way after sunset and way outside the rules of battle, these three survivors—Ashwatthama, Kripacharya and Kritavarman—attacked the Pandava camp. Desperate to avenge the death of his father, Ashwatthama attacked the sleeping Dhrishtadyumna, kicking him and pummelling him to death, consequently denying him the right of a Kshatriya to die with a weapon in his hand. The terrible trio didn't stop at that. They slaughtered the sons of the Pandavas and Draupadi; possibly they were mistaken that they were killing off the Pandavas or perhaps they were just plain evil.

Draupadi raged and raved when she found out. And the Pandavas were wild with grief and fury. A sort of battle was resumed. Ashwatthama called upon the very potent, very deadly Brahmashirshastra, and Arjuna retaliated by invoking his version of the same destructive weapon, which could destroy creation! It was somewhat like a nuclear bomb. This was followed by a stand-off, and all the gods begged the two to pull back from the

Read more about this in 'Heavenly Hardware, Bulletproof Beings', page 191.

brink or all creation would end. Arjuna accepted and ordered his weapon to withdraw. But Ashwatthama had never learnt how to! (Was he playing truant at the ashram?) So Krishna intervened and got the weapon directed at Uttara, wife of Arjuna's son Abhimanyu. Now, Uttara was pregnant and gave birth to a dead baby, but Krishna immediately brought him back to life. Phew! This baby was Parikshit, whom you read about just a few paragraphs earlier.

For his multiple crimes of infanticide and foeticide, Ashwatthama was at the receiving end of Krishna's fury. He was

cursed to live on and on till the end of this Kali Yuga, but in loneliness, in pain, in disease and in a state of total desolation. Bhima also pried out his magical gem, leaving a gaping wound that Krishna prophesied would never heal.

Ashwatthama still roams the mountains of north India, they say. If you live around there, he may just knock on your door at night, asking for some oil to soothe his wound.

A TIMELESS QUESTION

Why are only some people—these specific people—immortal? Think, think . . . Some religious texts have attempted to resolve this legendary loose end.

It is believed that some day Kali Yuga (this era, in which we exist) will brim over with so much sin, darkness and wrongful deeds, such immorality that Vishnu will take his final avatar and come riding in as Kalki on his snow-white horse Devadatta, brandishing his sword Ratna Maru. To undo evil and to shift the time to Sat Yuga, an era of goodness and peace, he will need to destroy all evil. For this, he will need to understand human nature, in both its forms, good and bad.

And it is *here* that the jigsaw gets completed. Each Chiranjeevi represents a human trait and/or skill, and has the final purpose to guide Kalki. For instance, Parashurama will emerge from Mahendragiri and guide Kalki on how to actually use that Ratna Maru, among other celestial weapons. So, basically, the immortals are lurking about, holding on to their magical powers, waiting for Kalki.

When he does, what do you think will happen to the Chiranjeevis?

THE MATHS OF MYTH

It is said in the Vedas that before the universe is created, Lord Vishnu is asleep in the ocean of all causes, the ocean of milk, Kshirsagar. His bed is a giant serpent with thousands of cobra-like hoods. While Vishnu is asleep, a lotus sprouts from his navel. Inside this lotus, Brahma is born. In the blink of an eye, Brahma awakes, lives a hundred years and dies. The lotus withers and falls apart. Another lotus sprouts, another Brahma is born, lives, dies . . . The process occurs on a loop.

We then learn that Vishnu is contained within a bubble. When the bubble pops, Vishnu disappears. As we pull out of this view, we see that there are many, many, many bubbles on the ocean surface. In each one of them is a Vishnu, and from each Vishnu's navel sprout the lotuses within lotuses within lotuses—like the first one we saw. In each moment, these bubbles form and pop. A lifetime in a moment. Eternity. Forever. In a blink. Time.

Brahma lives for 100 years.

Each year has 360 days or kalpas.

1 kalpa = 14 manvantaras

1 manvantara = 71 *mahayugas*

1 mahayuga = Krita + Treta + Dwapar + Kali

Krita Yuga = 17,28,000 solar years

Treta Yuga = 12,96,000 solar years

Dwapar Yuga = 8,64,000 solar years

Kali Yuga = 4,32,000 solar years

One mahayuga = 43,20,000 solar years

One manvantara = 30,67,20,000 solar years

Currently, we are in the 28th mahayuga of the 7th manvantara.

So, creation is 6 × 30,67,20,000 + 27 × 43,20,000 + 17,28,000 + 12,96,000 + 8,64,000 + 5112 = 1,84,03,20,000 + 11,66,40,000 + 38,93,112 = 1,96,08,53,112 years old.

Now that you have read these interesting, timeless, ageless tales, can you solve the clues and fill up the crossword? Some of these may require you to do some independent research or look through other chapters and sections in this book.

1. (Across) Though Hanuman was a Brahmachari, he met this son of his when he went to Patala to rescue Rama and Lakshmana (11)

(Down) Ultra-smart young rishi who worshipped Shiva with such devotion that the god saved him from Yama (10)

2. Animal named Ashwatthama killed by Bhima to fool Dronacharya into thinking his son was dead (8)

3. Son of the sage Richika and father of Parashurama, he met his end at the hands of the Haihayas (9)

4. King Kalayavana chased Krishna into this sage's cave, saw a sleeping figure, thought it was Krishna, kicked him rudely . . . and got blasted into a heap of ashes! (9)

5. The festival in Kerala that celebrates Mahabali's annual visit to his people and his land (4)

6. The mountain peak that Hanuman brought back when he couldn't locate the Sanjeevani herb to cure Lakshmana (9)

7. Son of sage Sharadvan and preceptor or guru of King Parikshit at the beginning of Kali Yuga (11)

8. A name given to Parashurama, due to his descent from Bhrigu, one of the Prajapatis created by Brahma (8)

9. The Pandava who went to Lanka as part of the *rajasuya yagna* performed by Yudhishthira, and was welcomed by Vibhishana with gifts (8)

10. Vibhishana's wife, who protected Sita as much as she could during her captivity in Lanka (6)

11. Son of Brahma, he was a follower of Rama and a father-in-law of Krishna (8)

12. Son of rishi Parashara and Satyavati (later empress of Hastinapura), he was called Krishna at birth (3,5)

13. Rama's great devotee, who was turned into a crow by the sage Lomas, is said to have been the first to recite the Ramayana (3,9)

5

BINARY BEINGS

Tales of Twins from Mythologies

Since ancient times, multiple births have fascinated people and inspired stories. Indian myths, too, are peppered with tales of twins, such as that of the inseparable Ashwins. And, more often than not, these tales focus on the twins' deep love and mutual loyalty.

Twice as nice, or double the trouble? Across mythologies in different cultures, twins (deities, humans and even beasts) are linked with the idea of something magical, something superhuman. They may have positive or negative stories. Their tales may be about sibling rivalry or unmoving loyalty. Twinship could be about being opposites like yin and yang, or perhaps about being two parts that fit perfectly to make a whole. Let's meet some legendary dual beings.

ASHWINS, TWINS OF LIGHT

In Hindu myths, the Ashwin twins are horse-riding healers. (If you know or learn the Sanskrit word for 'horse', you will see how apt their name is.) They are often depicted with human bodies and equine heads. With their father Surya for company, they perform an important duty: they travel across the entire sky in a gold chariot pulled by horses or swans. Within a day, they traverse the cosmos, removing darkness and bringing sunlight and warmth. Since they arrive before Surya, they personify the twilight, just before sunrise and after sunset.

Rapid, skilled and mighty, they are doctors to the gods and experts at Ayurvedic medicine. They save people in trouble, as they bear gifts of food, children, riches, light, happiness, victory and long lives. They can even bring the dead back to life and restore sight to the blind. These bros hate evil spirits, diseases and vices such as envy. The handsome demigods are themselves the youngest of all deities, glowing with health and vigour. It is

said that even their gold chariot appears tarnished next to their burnished beauty.

So who were these amazing brothers? The story goes that Surya's wife Saranya-Sanjana (you will meet them again in this chapter) simply couldn't bear how hot he was (!) and escaped in the form of a mare. Well, Surya wasn't one to take a hint. He turned into a horse and found her. They had two children, Nasatya and Dasra, popularly known as the identical Ashwin twins. Further along, in the Mahabharata, Pandu's second wife Madri is granted a son by each Ashwin and begets the twins Nakula and Sahadeva, two of the famed Pandavas.

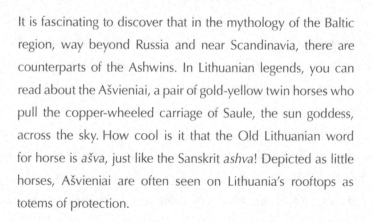

CULTURAL CROSSOVERS

It is fascinating to discover that in the mythology of the Baltic region, way beyond Russia and near Scandinavia, there are counterparts of the Ashwins. In Lithuanian legends, you can read about the Ašvieniai, a pair of gold-yellow twin horses who pull the copper-wheeled carriage of Saule, the sun goddess, across the sky. How cool is it that the Old Lithuanian word for horse is *ašva*, just like the Sanskrit *ashva*! Depicted as little horses, Ašvieniai are often seen on Lithuania's rooftops as totems of protection.

MYTHIC MEDICS

Christian lore takes us to third century Arabia, where twins Damian and Cosmas, wonderful healers, appeared in the dreams of the sick to restore their health. Renaissance-era illustrations suggest that they were the world's first transplant surgeons: they amputated a young boy's cancerous leg and grafted a black man's leg on to the stump. Because these miraculous medics never charged any fees, they became so popular that some jealous doctors accused them of converting their patients to Christianity. The Romans, who were persecuting Christians, tortured and beheaded them. How tragic! Ironically, their death only gave birth to greater fame. In the following centuries, they became known as saints, with churches even in Rome! They are celebrated as patron saints of twins and doctors. Some scholars believe this legend to be a Christian adaptation of the Greek myth of twin half-brothers and people's protectors, Castor and Pollux, whose eternal love we can still see as the two brightest stars in the constellation Gemini (which by the way is Latin for 'twins'!).

NAKULA AND SAHADEVA, TWINS OF INSIGHT AND FORESIGHT

As sons of the Ashwins (invoked by Pandu's wife Madri), the human princes with divine powers, Nakula and Sahadeva, are called Ashvineya, sons of Ashwins. They are perhaps the least known Pandavas, but certainly not the least important. In fact, in their story we learn a vital lesson: not everyone on a team can be a superstar; some people also strive behind the scenes for the team's success.

From the Ashwins came their legacy of medical expertise. Both were also brilliant swordsmen and made a big dent in Kaurava personnel during the big war. While planning to declare himself a Chakravarti Samrat or 'emperor of emperors', Yudhishthira asked the twins to conquer regions of Jambudwipa, much larger than Arjuna and Bhima's conquests. Apparently, they won not in the battlefield but in the mind. So skilled were they at diplomacy that they hardly met resistance, even from their fiercest rivals.

At an individual level, Nakula was amazing at breeding and training horses, and an expert in Ayurveda. In fact, in the thirteenth year of the Pandavas' exile, he assumed the role of the ostler Granthika, or Jayasena, in the Matsya Kingdom, caring for horses in the royal stable. He was also strikingly good-looking (often being compared to Kamadeva) and quite the strategizing statesman. It was on his advice that, when trying to make peace with Duryodhana, Yudhishthira asked for five villages. Nakula's plan was to surround the Kaurava capital Hastinapura from all sides, but it did not work because Duryodhana didn't agree.

Sahadeva's administrative acumen was equally formidable and, like Nakula, he too was equipped with knowledge of medicine (especially veterinary), along with equestrian and sword skills. Yudhishthira believed he was as intelligent as Brihaspati, teacher of the gods, and asked him to be his private counsellor. However, what set Sahadeva apart was that he was described as 'the most handsome of men' and his acumen in astrology was unmatched.

Now let us take a few steps back in time. There is a somewhat morbid sub-story in the Mahabharata about how Pandu, enlightened through years of meditation, instructed his sons to eat his flesh when he died and thus absorb all knowledge assimilated in his body. Imagine that! Initially, the brothers couldn't bring themselves to partake of the pater . . . but for the curious Sahadeva. One bite, and he knew all about the cosmos: past, present, future. In that moment, he would have 'precogged' and could have averted the great war of Kurukshetra . . . But then, what's a good tale without a caveat or warning?

Enter the Supreme Being with the warning that should Sahadeva ever use this all-powerful ability, his head would go kaboom into thousands of bits! (Ahem, was it not bursting already with all those yottabytes of data?) Well, the hapless Sahadeva could never share what he knew and never warn anyone. (Imagine his inner turmoil!) All that silence allowed him to figure out that one could actually predict the future by paying close attention to the goings-on in the world(s) around them. So what he did was develop the science of astrology, hoping to nudge some people towards some inevitable truths.

In fact, it is said that the Kauravas consulted the 'astrologer' Sahadeva about the most auspicious time or mahurat to begin

the great war of Kurukshetra and thus ensure their victory. Let's imagine that he did advise them and, at the given time, all the great warriors in the Kaurava faction were poised to attack . . . Meanwhile, Arjuna was having his crisis of conscience on the battlefield, wondering how he could attack and kill his own cousins, his kith and kin. Did Krishna give him the lengthy sermon we now know as the Bhagavad Gita to foil Duryodhana's astutely synchronized battle plan? Only Sahadeva would know the answer to that, we guess.

LAVA AND KUSHA, TWINS OF INTRIGUE

In the other great epic of the land, the Ramayana, we meet Lava and Kusha, Sita's twin sons. Those of you sensitive to gender issues would have questioned the episode of Sita's *agni pariksha*, and you should. Remember the challenge Rama faced: should he pay heed to fake news or stand up to popular opinion? We encourage you to debate it with friends, family and teachers.

So when Sita was pregnant and back in isolation in the woods, Valmiki's ashram became her home. Some legends say that Sita gave birth to twins who were fortified (in Achilles- or Karna-like manner) against ghosts. Valmiki did so with mantras and grass, and named them Lava and Kusha. He educated and trained them in military skills, especially archery—they could launch arrows at the speed of sound.

But what's mythology without mystery? Other legends say that Sita had only one child, Lava. One day, she requested Valmiki to babysit him while she bathed, but he was so engrossed

in his writing that she decided to take the child along and, as usual, multitask. When the absent-minded sage realized that the infant was nowhere to be seen, he pulled out a clump of kusha grass and breathed life into it. So there was an organically crafted 'Lava' cooing away when Sita returned with, ahem, the original Lava! The rishi renamed Lava #2 as Kusha, for the grass, and ordered Sita to raise both as her own. Interesting, yes, but it messes up the twin theory. Some accounts do conjecture at cloning, which would explain the twinning, but where would Valmiki get the DNA from?

On another note, since we spoke about Valmiki's writing, he composed 24,000 verses of the Ramayana and taught Lava and Kusha to sing them. In the *Uttara Kanda*, he emphasizes: 'I tell you the truth, O Rama, that these irrepressible twin brothers are your sons, O descendant of Raghu. Far from speaking untruth, it does not even spring up in my mind. I therefore know the truth that these twins are thy sons.' Elsewhere, he calls them *bimbadivotthitau bimbau ramadehattathaparau*, or 'two reflections of one original object; who came from the body of Rama, separately'. Clearly, he is affirming that they were identical twins.

Let us press fast-forward, and skip some years during which the young twins captured Rama's Ashwamedha horse, defeated their uncles in battle, faced off against their father, mellifluously sang the thousands of verses Valmiki had made them memorize, won over the denizens of Ayodhya and grew up into able administrators. After Rama, the twins ruled jointly, Kusha from Kushavati and Lava from Sravasti. It is believed that Kushavati still exists as Kasur, near Lahore in Pakistan, and that Lava founded a

new capital called Lavapuri, which is modern-day Lahore (from 'Loh', a variation of 'Lava'). Inside the famed Shahi Qila of Lahore still exists a non-functional temple, apparently dedicated to Lava.

LAKSHMANA AND SHATRUGHNA, TWINS OF LOYALTY

In the Ramayana, we don't learn much about the time spent together by that other set of twins, Lakshmana and Shatrughna, uncles to Lava and Kusha. They are the sons of Sumitra, who fed twice from the prasad of the *putrakameshti yagna*. Their sibling saga is overshadowed by the larger-than-life brotherhood of Rama and Lakshmana. However, the Puranas do tell us that while Rama is Vishnu's avatar, his brothers Bharata, Lakshmana and Shatrughna manifest as Shankha, Sheshanaga and Sudarshana Chakra, respectively. So, it may not be dwelt upon, but these twins share a cosmic connect.

And from what we observe, they shared an unwavering bond of loyalty to elder brother Rama. We know how Lakshmana followed Rama into exile, how he disfigured Surpanakha in a fit of rage when she insulted Sita and Rama, how seriously he took his duty as their sentinel, not sleeping a wink for fourteen years and thus earning the moniker Gudakesh, 'he who has defeated sleep'. (This comes in very handy in the war because Ravana's mighty and much-booned son Meghnad, or Indrajit, could only be defeated by someone who had not slept for twelve years.)

Back in Ayodhya, when Rama was exiled, no one was furiouser than Shatrughna. Enraged at the machinations of Manthara, the royal attendant responsible for this turn of events,

he pounced on her in the royal garden as she preened in Kaikeyi's gifts of glamorous clothes and jewels. He would have killed her had Bharata not intervened to remind him it was a sin to kill a woman, and would anger Rama no end.

When Bharata could not convince Rama to return to rule, he refused to take the throne himself either. Instead, he installed Rama's *padukas*, or slippers, on the throne and lived like a hermit by the Sarayu river. So, it was Shatrughna who administered the kingdom, with his three brothers in diverse forms of 'exile'. And eventually, when Rama knew his work on Earth was done and walked into the Sarayu to merge with his eternal Mahavishnu form, all his siblings followed in his footsteps, right into the fluid forever.

DRAUPADI AND DHRISHTADYUMNA, TWINS OF DARKNESS

Did you know that Draupadi, Mahabharata's most famous female character, had a twin brother named Dhrishtadyumna? They were, literally, borne by fire! Think of it as a symbol of the love-hate relationship between their father Drupada and his pal Drona. As young boys in the ashram of Bharadwaja (Drona's father, by the way), they had promised each other great loyalty and lifelong friendship, all of which faded with time. Poverty-stricken Drona asked Drupada to give him half his kingdom, as had been promised in those youthful dreams, but was firmly rejected.

Later on, Drona did manage to secure that coveted half by getting his disciple Arjuna to conquer it. With *half* his kingdom but *double* his rage, Drupada performed a *putrakameshti yagna* to obtain a son who would kill Drona. (Interestingly, this sacrificial rite was performed by rishi brothers Yaaj and Upyaaj, though it is not clear if they, too, were twins.)

Out of the sacrificial flame emerged a boy, his body the hue of fire, bow and arrow in hand. That was Dhrishtadyumna, 'the bold and the splendorous'. But wait . . . then there was a symphony of mantras and a girl appeared, divinely dark, her lustrous hair billowing about her, unscathed by flames. This was Krishna, a.k.a. Draupadi. (Did you know this?) A heavenly voice declared that she would cause the end of many, many Kshatriyas while the boy would kill Drona. D and D are a rare pair whose origin is based in hate, in negativity, in anger.

YAMI AND YAMA, THE ORIGINAL TWINS

Yami and Yama, twin children of sun god Vivasvat and cloud goddess Saranya-Sanjana, were siblings to the Ashwins. In Vedic tradition, they were the first-ever mortals or humans, and went on to create the human race, somewhat like Adam and Eve. Because he embodied all that was right and proper, Yama was also called Dharmaraj. When invoked by Pandu's wife Kunti, he blessed her with a son, the prince Yudhishthira, who later earned the same moniker.

Yami had immense affection for her sibling. Whenever Yama visited her, she would pamper him and ply him with fabulous

food. He granted her the boon that she would be worshipped as a deity; any brother and sister who bathed together in her sacred waters would be forgiven all their sins. It is to commemorate these twins that some of us celebrate Bhai Dooj on *yamadvitiya* (the second day after Diwali).

But wait, what is this about the River Yamuna? You see, Yama was also the first human to die and enter the afterworld, thus becoming the god of death and justice. Heartbroken at losing her beloved brother, Yami wept without pause, and her tears collected to become the raging Yamuna.

The gods couldn't bear to see her cry. So, they invented night to follow day and created the cycle of time, the greatest healer. One could say that Yami, or Yamini the night goddess, connects dusk to dawn and brings hope after grief.

TIME CAPSULE

In Jain mythology, time is a never-ending circle, with the world's well-being index transitioning from very-very sad (Dukham Dukham Kal), gradually through six phases, to very-very good (Sukham Sukham Kal), and then regressing, then evolving again, and so on . . . Interestingly, in the Sukham-squared era of absolute happiness, with wish-fulfilling trees, all children are born as twins, a boy and a girl. Pen down your thoughts: How can this phenomenon be seen as the most basic form of cosmic balance of energies?

YIMA AND YIMEH, THE PRIMEVAL TWINS

Time for a prehistoric crossover. Parallel to Rig Veda's Yama and Yami, in ancient Persian myth appear Yima and Yimeh, the primeval twins, children of Vivahvant, also a solar divinity. The spotlight here is more on Yima. In the *Avesta*, Yima is Jamshid, deriving from 'Yima Khshaeta' or 'Yima the radiant'.

Legend has it that Ahura Mazda, the supreme spirit, appeared to Yima and announced his mission, should he choose to accept it: 'Create the human race on Earth!' And like Ethan Hunt, he accepted this objective. He was not only the first man but also the first king, and such a virtuous one that his reign had no misery, no disease, no natural calamities . . . till a terrible white winter was predicted. So quite like the Biblical Noah who sheltered all creatures in his ark, Yima constructed a safe, self-sustaining *wara* or fortress to protect samples of each species from either an extremely long winter (Ice Age?) or a world-ending flood. Once the danger was over, they all emerged to repopulate Earth.

Did we tell you that the creation myth in Zoroastrianism also hinges on twins? While giving form to the universe, Ahura Mazda was quite sure that nothing can be all good all the time, so he first created the twin spirits Spenta Mainyu (whose instinct was to create, and align with truth, light, life) and Angra Mainyu (whose instinct was to destroy, and align with untruth, darkness, death). Cosmic balance is maintained through the struggle of these opposed spirits, and manifested for humanity as the eternal choice between good and evil.

In some versions, Zurvan, or the god of time, is actually the father of twins Ormazd and Ahriman, the former (another embodiment of Ahura Mazda) being beneficent and the latter maleficent, controlling the universe by turns, till Ormazd eventually wins.

THE BUDDHA'S TWIN MIRACLE

It is said that when the time came for the Buddha to leave Earth, he was in Kushinagar. He lay down in lion posture between two tall twin trees of shala or sal (*Shorea robusta*), his head pointing north. He had come full circle: he was born under the same tree, eighty-one years ago. In Lumbini, Queen Mahamaya and her companions were playing Shalabhanjika, which was literally 'bending shala' branches to pluck flowers and fling at each other. As she stood in *tribhanga* posture, clasping a bough, she gave birth to baby Siddhartha. Now, back under his birth tree, as the Buddha entered the state of *parinirvana*, a pair of trees from east and west stretched towards each other and linked, as did a pair from north and south, together forming a protective canopy over his body.

But enough talk of endings. Let's go back about thirty years from the above episode and relive a mind-boggling one. Six of the Buddha's rival philosophers, led by Purna Kasyapa, would constantly challenge him to a showdown of miracles. (Talk about having a weird hobby.) Finally, he assented on the condition that he would decide when and where. However, he was quite elusive; he would agree to a time and place, but then move to another city, over and over, giving sermons and gathering thousands of disciples: kings, courtiers, commoners alike. His competitors did not want to let him get away, so they followed him with their own 90,000 followers. Basically, the entourage just kept getting larger and larger. Can you guess what he was trying to do?

Finally, in Shravasti, in a massive hall with seven thrones, on the new moon of the first month of spring (now called Losar, or the Tibetan New Year), the Buddha arrived in a most dramatic manner, whizzing through the air, flying high above the heads of the others. Out of thin air appeared a jewelled path and the Buddha stood on it to perform the *Yamaka Patihariya* or the 'twin miracle' of contrasting phenomena.

His upper body erupted into flames even as a torrent of water gushed out of his lower body. Then the reverse happened, and fire and water sprang alternatively from the right and left side of his body. With this incredible chain of reactions, the hall was burnt to the ground but also promptly recreated as a transparent palace.

Everyone there—doubters and believers—was awestruck. And the Buddha didn't stop. For the next fifteen days, he conjured up unbelievable coups: he pushed a twig into the ground and out sprang a gigantic fruit-laden tree; he crafted twin jewelled mountains and lakes; he enabled people to read each other's minds; he invoked showers of rain such that only those who wanted to get wet did, others did not. He sent out 84,000 rays, one from each pore of his body, and filled the universe with light; at the tip of each bloomed a lotus, and on each lotus sat a buddha, teaching the tenets of Dhamma. Talk about multitasking! While stunning people with his fantastic feats, the Buddha was

also preaching, and not just in that hall but also in the heavens that he time-travelled to.

Not only did he vanquish his opponents but he also blessed all who listened to him with faith. It is said that 200 million beings understood the Dhamma because of the twin miracle!

LINGO BINGO

In Jain cosmology, Yamaka (Sanskrit for 'twin') is a twin mountain, near which flow the rivers Sita and Sitoda, in the Videha region of Jambudwipa, which is the most important continent because it is home to humans. Do you see echoes (Sita, Vaideha, Jambudwipa) from the Ramayana, and therefore Hindu myth?

TWO MUCH OR TOO MUCH?

Mythologies and folklore across India—in fact, the world—are peppered with appearances of twins. Be they deities or legendary humans, heroes or villains, siblings or cousins, they crop up all the time. If we break down the concept to its very basic form, they represent either the dual or opposite nature of the universe or the perennial battle between good and evil, both being ways to

maintain the overall entropy of the cosmos. In Greek legend, twin gods Apollo and Artemis governed sun and moon; in Zoroastrian tradition as we just read, good spirit Spenta Mainyu battled his destructive twin Angra Mainyu; and, in the Far East, the Chinese symbol of yin and yang is a depiction of opposing energies that together maintain the balance of nature.

The *Agni Purana* tells us of Kripa and Kripi, who were born to rishi Sharadvan and apsara Janapadi and abandoned on the forest floor. Adopted by King Shantanu (great-grandfather of Kauravas and Pandavas), they grew up to be scholars. Kripi married sage Dronacharya and Kripa became Kripacharya, a Chiranjeevi, a survivor of the Mahabharata war and counsellor to the Kauravas and Pandavas, the latter for generations.

Another set of twins produced by an apsara (Adrika) and a human (King Uparichara Vasu of Chedi) was that of Satyavati and Matsya. Misogyny alert. (Which means time to reflect, guys!) While the *putr* was acknowledged as the royal heir, the *putri* was left at the mercy of fisherfolk. Nevertheless, she went on to wed Shantanu of Hastinapura, the focal point of the face-off between the Kauravas and Pandavas. But that's another tale for another time.

Among mythical twins, often one is divine and the other human. Vishnu's dual incarnation as Nara and Narayana, twin sages from the Bhagavata Purana, is a fine example. They are basically Vishnu in a double role in a 'Dharma' production, where the villain is the demon with a thousand armours, Sahasrakavacha (later reborn as Karna). Owing to their intense meditation at Badrika, they were so powerful that even Shiva's mighty Pashupatastra fell like a blade of grass in their presence. The redoubtable rishis reappear in the Mahabharata, not as twins

but nearly inseparable cousins. Says Krishna (Narayana) to Arjuna (Nara): 'O invincible one, you are Nara and I am Hari Narayana, and we, the sages Nara-Narayana, have come to this world at the proper time.' (And now you can figure out the Karna connection.)

Speaking of Krishna, the sublime schemer . . . When Magadha's founder king Brihadratha married the twin princesses of Kashi, they bore, um—*weirdness alert*—two halves of a human body. Thankfully, the halves joined (owing to the hunger and foolishness of the witch Jara) to become whole, as Jarasandha, who went on to become a formidable ruler and Krishna's arch-rival. His gruesome end came at the hands of Bhima, who literally split him down the middle, back into two parts.

The mention of Bhima reminds us of a story from Telugu folklore, which tells us how his half-demon son Ghatotkacha used maya and disguise to help his cousin Abhimanyu (son of Arjuna) elope with his childhood sweetheart Sasirekha, aka Vatsala (daughter of Balarama). How does this fit into our tale of twins? Well, when the Pandavas lost their kingdom in the notorious game of dice, Balarama decided that Abhimanyu was too poor for his daughter, and had her engaged to his excellent student Duryodhana's son, Lakshmana Kumara.

Yes, Lakshmana Kumara and Lakshmanaa were twins, son and daughter of the eldest Kaurava. Lakshmana Kumara (who, in fact, did not finally marry Sasirekha, and we will read more about this soon) was a proficient archer, who fought valiantly in the Kurukshetra war where he was slain by the even greater archer, Abhimanyu. As for the twin sister Lakshmanaa, well, she was all set to pick the man she loved, Vrishasena (Karna's son), at her swayamvara, but Krishna's son Samba was also infatuated with

her. So he swooped in to abduct and marry her! Safe to say the myths are not big on gender equality, huh?

Elephant-headed god Ganesha is at times considered an eternal bachelor, and at others 'married' to—yep, you guessed it right—twins Riddhi and Siddhi. As per the Ganesha and Shiva Puranas, Riddhi (or Buddhi) personifies prosperity (or wisdom) and Siddhi spirituality. They mothered, respectively, Labha ('profit') and Kshema ('prosperity'), which some of you may know from pujas as Shubh-Labh. That Ganesha is referred to as *siddhi-buddhi-samanvita* (followed by siddhi and buddhi), meaning that when Ganesha is around, you are bound to think smart and make profits too!

Was it a 'smart' choice that demigod doorkeepers Jaya and Vijaya made when, having refused entry to the Kumaras (sons of Brahma) at the gates of Vaikuntha, they were cursed with time-bound banishment from heaven and faced a catch-22 dilemma: did they want seven earthly births as Vishnu's devotees or three as his enemies? They chose the latter, hoping for swift re-entry into celesto-sphere, and were reborn as brothers beyond borders. So, in Sat Yuga, they were the terrible twins Hiranyaksha and Hiranyakashipu, to vanquish whom Vishnu had to take two avatars of the boar Varaha and the man-lion Narasimha. In Treta Yuga, they were asura brothers Ravana and Kumbhakarna, slain by Ram. And, finally, in their last incarnations in Dwapar Yuga, they were cousins Shishupala and Dantavakra, killed by Krishna. (Some people believe that Kala Yuga saw them appear as boorish Brahmins Jagai and Madhai, who were taught a lesson in divine love by Chaitanya, another form of Vishnu or Krishna.)

Now that we are done learning about mythical twins, are you ready to put your twin powers of recall and research to use? Here is an interesting acrostic for you, where you get clues to arrive at a number of words. Once you've filled in all the letters for clues 1 to 7, #8 will emerge, like magic! That's what fills in the blank in the info nugget at the end. Let's go!

CLUES

1. Previous birth of the Buddha, as shown in the Jatakas; or one who seeks awakening and is on the path to become a buddha; a buddha-to-be
2. The half-man and half-beast avatar of Vishnu that burst out of a pillar to slay the demon at dusk on the threshold
3. Divine conch, the sound of which flagged off the Mahabharata war, and of which Bharata was a reincarnation
4. Equestrian rite, performed by a king to become Chakravarti; shown on a fourth century CE coin by Samudragupta

5. Once a valiant queen, she (mis)used her boons to give one son royal privilege and another, years of sylvan austerity

6. Priest to whom Ahura Mazda appeared in a vision; his namesake is the title character of a novel by Nietzsche

7. Four Brahma-Viharas of Buddhism: love (metta), compassion (karuna), joy (mudita) and equanimity (_____)

8. (HIDDEN WORD) Born in 1811 in a Thai fishing village, Chang and Eng Bunker were _____ twins, who did not let their unusual condition limit them. They travelled to America, worked in theatre, got married to a pair of sisters and had twenty-one children!

Can you match the illustrations with related characters, events or concepts you just read about?

Ahura Mazda

Ashwins

Parinirvana

Jaya and Vijaya

Yin and Yang

Damian and Cosmas

6

FANTASTIC BEASTS AND HERE YOU FIND THEM

Creatures Great and Small from Our Myths

*Winged horses, tusked fish, shape-shifting snakes . . . Bovines
that provide endlessly, raptors that devour senselessly. Some
so colossal they block the sun, others so infinitesimal they defy
vision. No myth is complete without its fabulous creatures,
divine or demonic. Whether they arrive on the scene from
primordial material or divine actions, they are somewhat familiar
in appearance yet incredible in ability, helping us expand our
imagination beyond what is humanly capable.*

Krishna displays the fabulous Navagunjara (nine beings) avatar to Arjuna, in an episode from the fifteenth century Sarala Mahabharata, composed in Odia by Sarala Dasa.

This cannot be an earthly creature, thought Arjuna, instinctively reaching for his bow. What stood before him was unseen, unheard of. A rooster's head on a peacock's neck; a bull's hump on a lion's torso; legs of a deer, tiger, elephant; a serpent's tail; and a human hand holding a lotus—nine beings in one fantabulous form . . . Could it be divine? It is believed to be Krishna manifesting spectacularly to either reward Arjuna for completing his penance on Manibhadra Hill or, an eco-sensitive interpretation, to prevent him from razing Khandavaprastha to the ground. Realizing that a creature may not exist in human imagination but surely in god's creation, Arjuna bows to the infinite wisdom of the universe.

AIRAVATA, the magnificent white 'elephant of the clouds', vahana of divine king Indra, emerged during the Samudra Manthan, the churning of the ocean. He had many tusks on many trunks, perhaps sprouting them at will to accomplish divine duties, such as sucking water from the  underworld and spraying it into the clouds to help Indra defeat Vritra, the drought demon. When all was quiet in Devaloka, he stood guard at the entrance to Swarga. And when he strolled in the clouds, lightning and thunder.

Read more about him in 'Call of Deity: Legendary Warfare', page 164.

AZHI DAHAKA was an invincible, three-headed, six-eyed dragon created from Angra Mainyu's lies to destroy goodness. Its gargantuan wings could block out the sun. For a thousand years, he ruled tyrannically till Feridun, the great Persian hero-king, defeated him. On being struck by a mace, his body bled more snakes, which could infest the world, so it is said that he is still chained on Mount Damavand. He will finally break free and devour one-third of humanity before the hero Karsasp finally slays him.

BEHEMOTH was a super-creature made by Yahweh and endowed with bronze bones, ironlike limbs, a substantial belly rippling with muscles and the ability to drink up a river. Despite this incredible power, he didn't wreak havoc on humans, preferring to munch grass and laze under trees, like a diplodocus. Strongest during summer solstice, he roars so stridently that all other animals tremble with fear and lose their ferocity. He thus helps to keep weaker animals safe.

BURAQ was the noble white steed of lightning speed, who effortlessly carried the Prophet ﷺ from Mecca to Jerusalem to heaven. A creature of lore, she appears in various artworks with a woman's head, radiant mane, gem-laden crown, eagle's wings, peacock's tail and bejewelled throat. Some believe that the Prophet ﷺ climbed to heaven on a glittering ladder, having fastened Buraq to a wall. Today, we know it as the Buraq Wall or Wailing Wall.

GARUDA was a mighty, emerald-bodied, shape-shifting 'birdman', and Vishnu's heavenly helicopter whose flapping wings could cause hurricanes, halt the earth in its orbit and emit

Vedic chants. A Dhamma-protecting 'dignity' (mythical, symbolic animal) in Buddhism and watchful yaksha of Jain tirthankara Shantinatha, he personified wisdom and courage. Fearless yet also merciless, he despised snakes as he had to wage war with Indra and steal amrit from heaven to release his mother from slavery.

GAVAEVODATA was the original bovine (both cow *and* bull, interestingly), one of Ahura Mazda's earliest creations, dazzling white like the moon. Ahriman was enamoured of its splendour but, in a dope villainy move, also killed it. Ahura Mazda swiftly airlifted it to the moon for 'purification'. From its organs emerged all animal species; from its marrow, plants. So its soul transformed into the soul of livestock that feeds on—and fertilizes—Earth's vegetation, thus perpetuating life.

GIRIMEKHALA was an enormous elephant—supposedly 250 yojanas or 3000 km tall—mounted on whom demon-lord Mara hindered Gautama's meditation. In some myths, the powerful pachyderm had one very evil eye, which cast deadly curses. Unfazed by Mara's supernatural attacks, Gautama requested the earth to support his claim to enlightenment. When the earth resounded with 100, then 1000, then 1,00,000 rumbles, Girimekhala fell to its knees, felled by the elephantine strength of a future Buddha.

HAYAGRIVA was a horse-headed demon, with a boon that only another 'hayagriva' could kill him. He terrorized everyone till the gods made Vishnu lose his head, assume his equine-headed avatar and call it a neigh! Alternatively, demons Madhu

and Kaitabha stole the Vedas, without which Brahma couldn't create, so Vishnu manifested as Hayagriva, sang the Sama Veda to distract them and sneaked the books back. He didn't need to 'see' the Vedas, because he was knowledge itself.

HUDHUD was a hoopoe through which the ruler-prophet Sulayman communicated with the sun-worshipping Queen of Sheba, convincing her to embrace Islam. It reappeared as a spiritual master in Persian mystic Attar's twelfth-century poem *The Conference of the Birds* about a soul's journey to enlightenment (personified as Simurgh). Of the thousand birds, thirty make it—only to realize that they are the destination. Wisdom lies in them. (Fun fact: in Persian, *si* is 'thirty' and *murgh* is 'bird'.)

HUMA was a sacred bird, who constantly flew over Earth, never landing (hence, legless) and staying invisible to humans. If its shadow covered you, or you thought you spotted it, you were blessed for life. Ancient kings smartly included it in their portraits, hoping to make their reigns last forever. Anyone who tried to catch or kill it would die within forty days. It was believed to live very long, die in fire and regenerate.

KANTHAKA was the loyal stallion astride whom Gautama witnessed the Four Sights and escaped his palace. Being 30 feet long, Kanthaka effortlessly bounded over ramparts and across rivers. Dying of grief when Gautama left, he was reborn as a Brahmin, attended the Buddha's sermons and achieved enlightenment. According to the ancient Pali text *Lokapannati*, Ajatashatru hid the Buddha's relics inside a Kanthaka statue, which

Ashoka discovered two centuries later, guarded by prehistoric robots powered by a magical life force!

KARA were gigantic, shark-like fish, symbolizing fertility as they lived in the primordial, life-giving Vourukasha Sea. They had X-ray vision—fins down, the keenest sight of all underwater creatures—and such sharp senses that they could feel the slightest rise or ebb of water. They didn't need food as the spirit of creation itself nourished them. Two of them tirelessly circled Gaokerena, the healing Haoma tree of immortality, to protect it against frog- or lizard-like evil spirits.

LEVIATHAN was a 500-km-long, many-headed, light-emitting, fire-breathing sea monster with scaly armour. It could boil oceans, eat a whale a day, crush ships and devour seafarers, but it had horrible halitosis (what we commonly call bad breath) and also a weirdly specific phobia of gill-clogging worms. At first, Yahweh created a pair of Leviathans to showcase his might but, concerned that they could procreate and terrorize the world, he killed the female. Her meat will be served as a feast to the righteous in heaven.

MAKARA was a marine monster, fabulously composed with body parts of elephant, stag, crocodile, boar, seal, peacock and snake! Some believe it was a prehistoric dugong, dolphin or mugger. It was the mount of river goddesses Ganga and Narmada, sea god Varuna and, at times, love god Kamadeva. It guarded thresholds and gateways, and still does in Hindu and Buddhist temples.

Setting fashion trends in heaven was up its alley(gator?); many gods wear makara-shaped earrings called Makarakundalas.

MANOHARA was a graceful *kinnari*, a woman and swan amalgam, featured in the Jatakas as the princess that Sudhana of Panchala marries, loses, seeks out and wins back, just like all epic heroes do. She represents heavenly hybrids, musicians to the gods, often depicted with cymbals, flute and veena. Kinnaris and *kinnaras* exist in pairs, crooning like birds, wearing flower garments, feeding on pollen, generally being harmless. No wonder they were hunted and caged for royal entertainment.

MARDYKHOR (manticore) was a man-eating monster with a scarlet lion-like body, a human face with blue-grey eyes, triple rows of razor-sharp teeth, a scorpion's tail with spikes it shot (and promptly regrew) and impenetrable hide. It hid in tall grasses, lured men (even three at a time) with its flute- or trumpet-like crooning, paralysed them with toxic stings and devoured them whole, bones, clothes and all. It moved faster than anything and could kill anything except elephants. *Creepy!*

MUCHALINDA was a serpent who offered his own body to protect the Buddha. As per the *Vinaya Pitaka*, just weeks after nirvana, Shakyamuni's meditation was threatened by a week of incessant rain and storms. Promptly, Muchalinda emerged, coiling into a cocoon around the meditating monk and stretching his hood into a protective umbrella overhead. When the elements eased off, he uncoiled, transformed into a young man and returned to his palace, brimming with selfless joy.

NANDI, the sacred white bull, was Kailasa's gatekeeper; Shiva's loyal vahana, who handled his affairs; and chief of ganas. Echoing his master, four-armed and three-eyed Nandi is depicted as luxuriously ornamented, glowing like a thousand suns, while holding a trident and thunderbolt. It was Nandi who braved Indra's weapons and wrath with his Behemoth-like, diamond-tough body and lopped off Airavata's head for the headless Ganesha. He also knew all the latest bops because he did the soundtrack for the cosmic *tandava*.

A BIT OF HIS(S)TORY

PADMAVATI and **DHARANENDRA** are the half-human, half-serpent *yakshi* and yaksha (attendants) of Parshvanatha, the twenty-third Jain tirthankara. The *Kalpa Sutra* narrates how Prince Parshva once saved two serpents trapped in an ascetic's fire. Severely scorched, both were about to die, so Parshva recited the powerful Navkar Mantra and they passed away in peace. They were reborn as the queen and king of snakes, the latter a shape-shifting Nagakumara ruling over 6000 gods. As a cosmic-level return gift, they protected Parshva—by then a meditating monk—from demonic threats like stampeding elephants and torrential cloudbursts. They placed a large lotus under his feet to raise him over the flood, and fanned out their hoods to create a massive umbrella. Because they literally served the Jina, the ophidian duo was further reborn in heaven as divine attendants of Parshvanatha, who is always depicted with a canopy of seven, at times eleven, serpent hoods.

RE'EM was a Biblical unicorn, or perhaps an aurochs or rhinoceros because—horn. It was strong, swift, agile, untameable and possibly untrustworthy because—pride. One touch of its horn could detox and sweeten any water. Jews believe it dwarfed mountains and dammed the Jordan with its, erm, dung.

It couldn't fit in Noah's ark, so it was tied by its horn, allowing it to swim along and poke its mouth in to breathe and feed.

SAMPATI and **JATAYU**, Arun's colossal vulture sons, were truly Rama's 'wingmen'. In a brotherly flight contest, when young J flew too close to the sun with Icarus-like joy, elder bro S shielded him but got singed himself. Later, flightless in the forest, he spotted the Pushpak Vimana with the abducted Sita and informed the vanaras. Tragically, in trying to save his friend Dasharatha's bahu, Jatayu had moments earlier lost his wings and life to Ravana's sword.

SHESHANAGA, Vishnu's thousand-hooded, never-ending, multi-coiled snake float in the primordial sea, was born to Kashyapa

and Kadru. Meditating motionlessly while surviving on air, he impressed Brahma, who asked him to stabilize Earth. Sheshanaga did one better and supported all the planets on his heads. When he yawned, earthquakes occurred! When he uncoiled, creation happened; when he re-coiled, everything ended. Extremely loyal to Vishnu, he often reincarnated with him: Lakshmana to his Rama, Balarama to his Krishna.

SIMURGH was a benevolent bird deity with a canine head, lion's claws, often a human face, peacock plumage, healing feathers and copper wings so strong it could carry a whale. It lived atop Saena, the Tree of All Seeds. When it took flight, the branches shuddered and sent millions of seeds across the world, creating life. It lived for 1700 years—witnessing the world's destruction thrice and gaining endless wisdom—before diving, Phoenix-like, into flames.

SURABHI, or the holy cow **KAMADHENU** created in the Samudra Manthan, could fulfil her owner's every desire. For Vasishtha, whose hermitage she lived in, it meant an endless supply of ghee, milk and other foods. For Jamadagni, who owned her later, her abduction made his son decimate the Kshatriyas twenty-one times. Cloud-complexioned, woman-headed, vibrant-winged and peacock-tailed, she also symbolized the Vedas (legs), gods (horns), sun and moon (face), fire (shoulders) and the Himalayas (legs).

TAKSHAKA, the 'flying snake', Sheshanaga's sibling, bore serious grudges against the Pandavas. Arjuna had burnt down his Khandavaprastha habitat, slain his wife and forced him to relocate, so he yearned to fulfil destiny by killing Arjuna's grandson Parikshit, already cursed to a snakebitten end. Takshaka shape-shifted into a tiny worm to achieve this, inciting the wrath of Parikshit's son Janamejaya, whose *sarpa satra yagna* nearly annihilated the entire snake species till a truce was reached on Naga Panchami day.

UCHCHAIHSHRAVAS (yep, a tongue-twister this one) was a seven-headed flying horse, prototype of equines, described as the vahana of sun god Surya and demon king Bali but most famously as Indra's second mount. Emerging in the Samudra Manthan, it was milky-white, except when Kadru's thousand naga kids hid in its tail as black hairs, all to win a wager. Luminous like a supernova, it could gallop within minutes to all divine lokas—talk of horsepower!—and possessed spiritual inner hearing.

ZIZ was a colossal cosmic bird, whose feet rested in Earth's core and whose head touched the sky. Spreading her wings, she

could block the sun but also shield creation from tempests. She delighted God with her birdsong, but it wasn't enough to undo the 'rebellion' of controlling nature. She too will become food at the end of days, tasting a bit like this (*zeh*), a bit like that (*zeh*), which is why the name.

COSMIC TRAFFIC

What the gods like to ride, and why

Shiva rides the wise but untameable bull Nandi. Parvati rides the majestic lion, perhaps the only beast that can dominate the bull. (Yeah, down with patriarchy!) But why did the gods need these creature cars? Surely they could mind travel, teleport, osmote or simply fly. Turns out that vahanas are more than chariots, seats or companions. Often godlike or avatars themselves, they are indeed symbols of the deities whom they support as well as complete in a symbiotic manner. In cases where gods are not represented in identifiable human forms, then associated symbols like animals help us, like icons, to identify them. Vahanas also feature on divine flags. Since most of these are familiar beasts or birds, it is easy to relate to them.

While they highlight the deity's positive powers, they also symbolize negative threats that the deity defeats. When the *mushak* is squashed (literally) by the elephantine Ganesha, any negative attributes like mouse-like timidity or rodent-like destructiveness are subdued. Meanwhile, Ganesha's brother

Murugan (or Kartikeya) rides the flamboyant peacock Paravani, which was created when he split the demon Soorapadman into two. We see this as his victory over vanity, and the aspiration towards controlling one's own senses. That the peacock can crush a snake also depicts the crushing of fear. While *Pavo cristatus* also appears near Saraswati with its gorgeous plumage not on display (advising us to ignore external appearances and focus on internal truth), her chosen mount is the graceful *hansa* or swan, a creature that possesses *neera-ksheera viveka*, the intelligence to separate water (impurity) from milk (purity), propelling us away from illusion and towards reality. Similarly, with Lakshmi, the goddess of prosperity, comes her vahana Ulooka, the owl whose being near-blind by day is seen as single-minded focus on the real wealth of spirituality, and whose wide-eyed, unmoving gaze is the steadiness of a person who does not allow fortune to go to the head.

Some devis are not as tranquil though, and with good reason. Durga came to Earth to cut down Mahishasura, the half-buffalo-half-man patriarch giddy with power, but her focused ferocity needed the raw power of her lion, who bit and paralysed the asura, allowing her to gore him with her trident. In the case of Yama, god of death, his *mahisha* Paundraka signifies a strong sense of justice, with a focus on *strong*, because that's what he needs to be to ferry the lame Yama all around the world, looking for those whose time on Earth is ending, and then carry both back to Patala!

Beyond Patala and Swarga, beyond time and space reclines Vishnu on his loyal serpent Sheshanaga, but when

he rides, it is on the Garuda, the godlike vulture who is the snake's natural and most vicious foe. This interesting pairing of opposites echoes the harmony that Vishnu brings to creation in his role as the preserver. And then there is the god of wealth. Though he is also associated with the mongoose, wild boar, goat, even elephant, Kubera is the only deity who is shown riding a human and is called *naravahana*. Can you figure out why?

NAME GAME

Can you identify the following deity and vahana duos?

Agni	Parrot
Vayu	Donkey
Yamuna	Makara
Ganga	Tiger
Bhairavae	Tortoise
Ayyappan	Ram
Budhe	Antelope
Shani	Yali
Kamadeva	Dog
Shitala	Crow

DIY DEITY

What is your favourite animal? What qualities of this animal do you admire? Is there anything you do not like about it? Here is some space for you to draw or write about your chosen creature as a vahana, and then pair it with a deity, existing or imagined. Focus on the physical and spiritual features, the outfit and accessories, perhaps also the background . . . Go wild!

BEASTLY TALES

Here's a bunch of beastly questions to make you think, recall and research more. Pick the correct option.

1) In Buddhist legend, which horse-headed/shaped form does the bodhisattva Avalokiteshvara take to save the souls of men who are following the wrong path in life?
   a. Haihaya
   b. Ashvaghosha
   c. Mustang
   d. Valaha

2) Which son of Kadru agreed to be anchored to Mount Mandara and became the rope needed during the churning of the Ocean of Milk?
   a. Takshaka
   b. Sheshanaga
   c. Vasuki
   d. Kaliya

3) On Judgement Day will arise a fabulous beast with a bull's head and an ostrich's neck. With what will it mark the faces of true believers?
   a. Staff of Musa
   b. Ring of Sulaiman
   c. Cloak of Yusuf
   d. Lily of the Valley

123

4) What beastly form, with many legs and sharp claws, did Shiva assume to stop Vishnu's Narasimha avatar from destroying the world in his unstoppable rage?

a. Sharabha

b. Banjhakri

c. Kabandha

d. Mainaka

5) Like Greek legends have the flying horse Pegasus, Hindu myth has its own version, Devadatta. Which avatar of Vishnu has it for a mount?

a. Rama

b. Kalki

c. Parashurama

d. The Buddha

6) Which giant bird with a canine body and aquiline wings lives under the Tree of All Seeds and protects Persia (and the Parsi faith) against invaders?

a. Saena

b. Simurgh

c. Gryphon

d. Chamrosh

7

A LEAF OF FAITH

A Journey into Legendary Ecosystems

*Just like multiple mythologies have unique interpretations of
similar concepts, like good versus evil, and the same people
like a sun god or a goddess of knowledge, it is no surprise
that legendary ecosystems also overlap. However, the
representations and the deeper meanings may be different.
Let's go on a discovery of divine flora from myths: plants, herbs,
trees, flowers, fruit . . .*

IS IT A FLOWER? OR IS IT A TREE?
IT IS THE LOTUS!

In a fascinating Hadith in the Quran, the Prophet ﷺ describes his Mi'raj, or 'ascent into heaven', guided by the archangel Jibreel (or Gabriel in the Bible). A horse-like creature carried him all the way to Jerusalem in one night, where he rose to the heavens and returned, as a sign of his prophethood. During this jet-setting, he encountered the Sidrat al-Muntaha, 'Lote-Tree of the Farthest Boundary' with large yellow-red fruits like pitchers (which he ate as he descended to Earth) and even larger leaves, resembling elephant ears.

Its name reveals its role: it marks the boundary between the known world and the unknown, the *ghayb*, which is known only to Allah or the chosen one he tells it to. Basically, none can transcend it except the Messenger of Allah, the Prophet ﷺ. Rooted at the base of Allah's throne, it marks the end of all that rises from the land of mortals and the start of all that descends from the realm of divinity. The absolute tree of knowledge, a concept that recurs across myths and creation stories.

But what is this tree? This space-straddling specimen of arboreal awesomeness, scholars and scientists believe, is a kind of Mediterranean jujube from the *Ziziphus* genus: *Ziziphus lotus* (hence 'lote') or *Ziziphus spina-christi* (also called *sidr*). Its edible drupes boost energy, reinforce immunity and, it is believed, were used as medicine by ancient Egyptians. Early Bedouins, the nomadic tribes of the Levant, Arabian Peninsula and north Africa, valued its fruit highly. They would dry it in

large quantities for the winter, turn it into thick paste and shape it into bread.

THE BUSH THAT BLEEDS

In Christian tradition, however, the role of the lotus tree is quite contrary to 'curative' or 'nutritive'. Carefully read the scientific name: *Ziziphus spina-christi*. What does it mean? Literally, 'Christ's Thorn Jujube'. It is identified with the thorn bush, using the branches of which a crown was braided and placed on Jesus's head, before his Crucifixion. The crown of thorns was one of the 'instruments of the Passion', which his captors used to hurt and mock him, jeering away: 'Hail, King of the Jews!' Guess bullying is a concept as old as time.

According to animistic folklore of the regions to which it is native, Christ's Thorn Jujube groans with pain when it is cut and 'bleeds', thus giving rise to the belief that it has life, like humans. However, science tells us that the stone fruit (drupe) tree exudes, reddish sap to heal an injury. Well, in a way, it is a cry for help.

Goosebumps alert! In a place called Hatzeva Spring in Israel, there is a massive *Ziziphus spina-christi*, 14 m tall, 7 m around the trunk with boughs spanning 15 m. It is not only the region's largest tree but also the oldest known sample of the species, and has been dated to 1500–2000 years ago! People believe that this is the very tree from which Jesus's crown of thorns was made.

Let's take a quick detour back to an old Muslim legend about another sidr growing in paradise, this one with a more earthly purpose. It has as many leaves as there are humans! And on each leaf appears the name of a person. Every year, in the middle of the month of Ramazan, as the sun sets, this deathly *darakht* is given a thorough shake. *Jiggle-jiggle, wobble-wobble . . .* Any withering and unhealthy leaves start to loosen and drop to the ground. The names on the leaves that fall are of the people who will die in the coming year. Sounds ominous?

THE DRUPE OF DEVOTION

Now let's meet a cousin of the lotus tree, *Ziziphus mauritiana*, found as ber all over the Indian subcontinent. Especially in south India, it is one of the Sthala Vriksham, trees that are so important in temples that they too are worshipped. Shiva's devotees offer to him ber fruit, especially during Mahashivratri, or 'Great Night of Shiva', the origin of which is a matter of debate. Does it mark Shiva's cosmic tandava, or his marriage to Parvati or perhaps his swallowing of the *halahala* poison from the Samudra Manthan? We will read more about that soon but, for now, back to the ber.

Rich in medicinal and nutritional value, it is a symbol of good health, long life and wish fulfilment—who doesn't want all of those from their favourite deity? The ber often pops up in the Hindu epics. From the Ramayana, we know of the heart-warming incident in which Shabari, an untouchable old woman, meets the person she's been waiting for all her life. You see, she was

a queen called Malini in her former life but was cursed to be reborn as a Bhilni, a hunter woman, and exist as a social outcast till Rama un-cursed her. She was living out her days in sage Matanga's hermitage, tending to fragrant flowers until—as luck would have it—Rama and Lakshmana arrived, while searching for Sita. Shabari welcomed them respectfully with a basket of ber fruit, tasting each and offering only the ones that tasted sweet. Erm! L was not too happy about this, but R ate them graciously, acknowledging Shabari's devotion, and finally released her from her curse.

In the same search for Sita, the siblings met a ber tree, which told them—yes, the trees spoke—that it had tried to extricate Sita from Ravana's clutches as the Pushpak Vimana flew past. In the struggle, Sita's sari had got entangled in its branches, and a little swatch was still stuck there. When it pointed out the direction in which the abductor and abductee had gone, Rama blessed it with near-immortality: no matter how badly it is mangled, it will not perish; if even a single root remains, it will spring up again and flourish. And this is why the ber tree is hardy and can grow in arid areas like deserts.

A BER-RY TO MAKE YOU MERRY

And, sometimes, in a desert of hopelessness, it also shines bright. There is exactly such a legend in Sikh history, that of the Dukh Bhanjani Beri, or 'sorrow-removing tree', standing to this day in the central courtyard of Harmandir Sahib (Golden Temple), the Sikhs' most sacred space. It is a story of unwavering faith.

Around the time Guru Ram Das was developing the settlement of Amritsar, Bibi Rajni was devotedly ferrying her leprous husband on a pilgrimage. When they reached Amritsar, she set him down in the shade of a ber tree by a pool and went to look for food. On her return, he was nowhere to be found; instead, a healthy, able-bodied man claimed that he was her husband. Uh? Apparently, while she was gone, he saw two black crows fighting over a morsel of bread, which fell into the pool. Both swooped in and when they emerged, they had turned white! Okay, let's suspend our agitation at this contempt of body positivity, and imagine the amazement of the diseased man lying there and witnessing this 'miracle'. He promptly dragged himself over and dove straight into the pool, emerging healthy and, well, handsome.

Bibi Rajni was incredulous, and believed the tale only when Guru Ram Das vouched for the pool's power of healing. The happy couple embraced Sikhi and served under the guru to enlarge the pool and build places of worship. And just like X marks the treasure in adventure tales, the Dukh Bhanjani Beri—under which the leper sat—marks the spot where even now, people enter the Amrit Sarovar to wash away their pains and sorrows.

Having withstood centuries of war and weather, Harmandir Sahib still stands as a beacon of hope for millions of believers. Look up, right to the top, and there sits its low-fluted dome, gilded and resplendent, with the beautiful lotus petal motifs at the base. Here is where we arrive at the classic form of the 'lotus', as the flower that we know.

The symbolism of the lotus in Indian culture is known quite well. It is perhaps the single most popular object in traditional

Indian art, architecture, literature and mythology. Guru Nanak, the founder of Sikhism, frequently used the lotus metaphor— that it grows in muddy waters yet stays beautiful—in sermon and song.

Bimal majhar basis nirmal jal padman javal re
Padman javal jalras sangat sang dokh nahi re

(In the clear water resides the lotus and also slime
But the lotus remains unsullied by the dirty slime)

Nanak urged his followers not to give up the world but experience it wholly, fulfilling their duties while aspiring towards the divine: 'Just as the lotus in the lake is undisturbed by the water, just as the duck is not made wet by floating in water, in the same way, by linking one's consciousness with the Supreme Being, by uttering the holy name, one crosses the world ocean.'

LESSONS FROM THE LOTUS

Like Buddhist Zen master Thich Nhat Hanh says: 'No mud, no lotus.' Which means that we need to see sorrow before we can find true happiness. We must remove ignorance to reach the light. From another belief system, which is Buddhism, the same advice comes to us as the *Lotus Sutra*. It is the most important of all sutras (collections of Shakyamuni's teachings). Over twenty-eight chapters of rich descriptions of the cosmos and the Buddha's powers (for instance, he can show you thousand worlds in thousand directions, each with its own buddha), the *Lotus Sutra* tells us that each of us has the potential to be a buddha, an enlightened one. Buddhahood is simply the journey of recognizing

Read more about this in 'Binary Beings', page 97.

our inborn powers of wisdom, compassion and courage, while meaningfully doing what we choose to do: study, teach, sing, paint, heal, build, govern, cook, grow . . . whatever we desire.

The sutra's Japanese title and, in a way, its essence is contained in the popular chant *nam-myoho-renge-kyo*, reciting which is a way to awaken your inner buddha. When it germinates, the lotus is rooted deep in mud but slowly pushes its way through murky waters till it breaks surface, bathes in the sunlight and blossoms beautifully. We can appreciate this transformation as enlightenment, as rebirth, as winning against all odds.

The lotus, or *padma* in both Tibetan and Sanskrit, is not a random choice here. It represents the Buddha. Avalokiteshvara, buddha of infinite compassion (of whom the Dalai Lama is a form) is also known as Padmapani ('lotus bearer') and Shadakshari ('six-syllabled'). And those six syllables are *om mani padme hum*. This powerful mantra is often seen printed on prayer flags and wheels, carved into rocks, even painted on the sides of hills. Literally, it means 'jewel in the lotus', referring to the Buddha, but its spiritual meaning holds more importance: it is the core of all the wisdom of the Buddha, and chanting it is a way to unlock the buddha within.

The lotus is not just a symbol of the Buddha; it *is* the Buddha. Legend has it that Mahamaya, the Buddha's mother, conceived him in a dream, in which she ascended to heaven where a white elephant, holding a white lotus in its trunk, circled her thrice and

entered her womb. In fact, Siddhartha's birth is often shown via lotuses and another deity associated with it, the Hindu goddess Lakshmi. In the carvings in stupas at Bharhut and Sanchi (both in Madhya Pradesh), she is shown seated or standing on a lotus, holding in each hand a lotus, which is watered by two elephants. When the baby Buddha grew up and started to walk, it is said that a lotus would bloom everywhere he stepped. What a challenge that must have been for the royal gardeners in Suddhodana's mansions! Several columns and pillars built by Ashoka, the conquering emperor who gave up war and became Buddhist, were topped by an inverted lotus, or a lotus with its petals turned down, again symbolizing the Buddha's birth.

The lotus throne is another visible element and auspicious symbol in Buddhist art, especially painting and sculpture. You will see the Buddha, bodhisattvas and major deities either sitting or standing on a lotus in full bloom. Oh yes, that's important: the stage of blossoming. A fully open bloom represents enlightenment and self-awareness, a closed one represents a time before that state is achieved and a partially open one represents the journey towards enlightenment, for which one needs to take a leaf, oops, leap of faith.

Merciful goddess Tara, the feminine counterpart of Avalokiteshvara, was born from a lotus. In nearly all her depictions, she is seated on a fully open lotus, holding one or more lotuses, and with her right leg lightly resting on yet another lotus, ready to leap into action to help whoever needs her.

Given the encyclopaedic level of its significance, why would the Buddha not use the fab flower in his sermons? Once, when someone asked him if he was a god, he responded: 'Just like a red, blue or white lotus—born in water, grown in water, rising above water—stands unsmeared by the water, in the same way, I—born in the world, grown in the world, having overcome the world—live unsmeared by the world. Remember me, brahman, as *awakened.*'

Another story tells us that the Buddha once gave a silent sermon. No words. No miracles. No interaction. All he did was hold up a golden lotus. And Mahakashyapa smiled. And in that moment, the Buddha knew that his disciple had glimpsed enlightenment. Red, blue, white, golden . . . Get the drift? Yes, the colour of the lotus is also significant. And here's how:

Gold lotus: state of complete enlightenment
White lotus: purity of both mind and spirit
Pink lotus: the Buddha himself; history of all buddhas
Red lotus: love, compassion;
associated with Avalokiteshvara
Blue lotus: intelligence, logic, wisdom;
associated with Manjushri
Purple lotus: very rare, conveys many things, depending
on the number of flowers in a cluster

Remember the lotus-at-every-step legend of baby Buddha? Well, there are also 'footprints of the Buddha' found across Asia—relics that have been engraved in rocks—like a trail he left behind towards the treasure of enlightenment for each of us buddhas-to-be. Many of these contain within them a wheel-like sun with thousand spokes. This could be a sort of diagram of a lotus, which opens at dawn and closes at dusk.

ONE FLOWER, MANY FAITHS

Such a flattened lotus is also seen in rock-cut cave temples, especially in the impressive Ellora Caves, where Buddhist, Jain and Hindu temples have co-existed for centuries. If the Ajanta Caves are known for their murals depicting the Jataka tales, and featuring lovely lotus ponds, the ones at Ellora are more culpture-focused, and the lotus recurs as a motif, carved like a wheel in panels and ceilings. Is it because when you press a lotus flat, you can imagine its petals as spokes of a wheel? If we imagine further, the wheel of Dharma, in both Buddhism and Jainism, could actually be a geometric representation of a lotus.

In Jainism too, the birth of Mahavira involves omens in dreams. According to the *Kalpa Sutra*, an important Jain scripture composed by Bhadrabahu in the fourth century BCE and containing the life stories of all Jain tirthankaras, Queen Trishala had a series of fourteen or sixteen dreams, which together foretold what her child would be like and what he would achieve. The lotus appears in a few: in the fourth dream, Lakshmi arrives on a magnificent lotus throne, holding a lotus in her hand, signifying that the child will be prosperous; in the ninth, a pair of vases with lotuses appear, depicting compassion; in the tenth, there is a lake filled with lotuses, suggesting serenity and detachment from worldly possessions.

Now, as you would know, Jains have twenty-four tirthankaras, and they look quite similar, so each of them has a distinguishing emblem, like the lion for Mahavira, the last one.

The sixth, Padmaprabha, is depicted by a lotus, and the twenty-first, Naminatha, by a blue lotus. Just like Rishabha (the first) and Mahavira, he is said to have attained moksha in padmasana, the lotus position of yoga.

Before moving from Jainism to Hinduism, we must mention Vimal Vasahi, the eleventh century shrine to Rishabhadeva or Adinatha, one of the richly carved Dilwara Jain temples in Mount Abu, Rajasthan. Of its many carved ceilings, the most impressive—and the largest, spanning 25 feet across and rising 30 feet from the floor—is that of its pillared hall. It has a dizzying array of sculptures, like dancers, musicians and galloping horses, but the most pertinent here are the hundreds of lotuses in blossom, especially the twelve dangling around the central and largest lotus pendant, which tapers down like the grace of god reaching down to bless humans.

A BLOSSOM MOST BLESSED

Fortune and fertility,
Prosperity and purity
Highest consciousness
Life, divinity, eternity
Truth, auspiciousness, beauty
Satyam, shivam, sundaram

All these qualities, and more, are contained in the lotus symbol of Hindu mythology. The *Panchavimsha Brahmana* of the Sama

Veda says that the lotus is born of the celestial light of all the nakshatras (constellations).

In fact, in one creation story, a lotus stem peeked out from Vishnu's navel (hence his name Padmanabha), as he was resting on his snake-bed Ananta in the cosmic waters, possibly playing Earthville on his iPad(ma). From the stem emerged a Pundarika, or thousand-petalled lotus of pure gold, shimmering with the radiance of the nakshatras. As it bloomed, unfurling its pristine petals in supernatural slo-mo, out came Brahma, the demiurge who went on to create the universe. If you look at a classic illustration of four-armed Vishnu, there is a lotus in his lower right hand, and this represents the universe that has been generated— an entire cosmos of creation from formless fluid.

As per the *Shilparatna*, the classical sixteenth-century text that suggests ways to depict various entities in dance, drama, sculpture and painting, Ravi the sun god (we met him earlier as Surya and Vivasvat) must be lustrous like a golden lotus, must be seated on a red lotus and must always hold a fully blossomed red lotus in each of his two hands. Indeed, stories about the lotus abound in Hindu scripture, as do lotuses in stories! It was amid the fibres of a lotus stalk in Manasa Sarovar in the Himalayas that Indra—transforming, like Ant-Man into a microscopic Indra—hid to avert whatever punishment lay in store for his sin of having killed a Brahman.

In the Puranas, Kamadeva or the God of Love is an ecosystem unto himself, with a parrot for his vahana and a sugarcane for his bow. (We will read more about this in other chapters.) In his quiver

Read more about him in 'Heavenly Hardware, Bulletproof Beings', page 188.

full of flower-tipped arrows, there are two with lotuses: *aravinda* (white lotus) and *nilotpala* (blue lotus).

Do you remember the story of how Ganesha got his pachyderm pate? Well, when Brahma managed to fix the oversized head on to the child's body,

Read more about this in 'In the Name of the Father', page 203.

he also bathed him with water sprinkled from a Brahma Kamal, and that is how the elephant-headed god finally came to life and breathed his first, via a much elongated nose!

Like in Buddhism and Jainism, the lotus in Hinduism too is a throne for deities, such as Saraswati, Ganesha, Kubera, Ganga. In fact, Hindu texts go a step further and compare the deities and literally all their attributes to the lotus. The handsome Krishna is often called Kamalanayana. Duryodhana addresses him as Pundarikaksha. Rajeevalochana is what Dashratha calls his eldest son, Rama. All these names mean 'the one with lotus-like eyes'. In the Pahari school of miniature painting, Hindu deities—especially Krishna—are shown wearing pinnacled crowns surmounted by lotus buds.

In the case of Lakshmi, the goddess of wealth, things get somewhat out of hand. Not only does she stand or sit on a lotus (hence, Padmesthita), live in a lotus (Sarasijanilaya), hold lotuses in both her upper hands (Padmahasta, Padmini, Pushkarini) and wear lotus garlands (Padma Malini) but in some legends, she also emerges from a lotus on Vishnu's forehead (Padmasambhava or Padmavati), has a lotus complexion (Padmavarna), has a face like a lotus (Padmanana), has thighs like lotuses (Padma-Uru), has eyes like lotuses (Padmakshi) and, but of course, is also especially fond of the lotus (Padmapriya).

That is a lot(us) of names! (Wait till you start learning synonyms for this phenom of a *phool*: Pushkar, Nalin, Indivar, Ambuj, Neeraj, Pankaj, Jalaj, Jalodbhava, Sahasrapatra . . . Can you think of more?)

In meditation practices, the lotus denotes the highest level of enlightenment. In Ayurveda, the Sahasrara or the crown chakra is the focus of spiritual awareness and pure consciousness, and is called the 'thousand-petalled lotus'. In hatha yoga, those striving to reach the supreme consciousness held in this chakra (found at the top of the head) assume the lotus position or *padmasana*.

It is as if we have come full circle. In mythology, the lotus gives life to all beings and, in meditation, it takes those beings close to nirvana, where they stop being and merge with the supreme power. And then the world starts to spin again.

LOTUS TEMPLE:
AN ELEGY TO HUMANITY

The Baha'i faith, a young religion from mid-nineteenth century Persia, says that all faiths teach the same truth and should work together for the unity of all humanity. When the Baha'i community wanted to create a house of worship (*Mashriqu'l-Adhkar*) in New Delhi, open to one and all, they did not have to look far for inspiration. The lotus, deeply embedded in Indian culture, religion, myth, aesthetic and everyday life is also an important element in Persian and Zoroastrian art and architecture. Throw into this mix some numerology: nine, being the highest single-digit number, is significant for Baha'is as they believe it is perfect and complete. They often place a nine-pointed star in their temples. In the case of the Lotus Temple, the perfect nine and the meaningful lotus unite in an architectural masterpiece of white marble. It appears like a floating lotus on the verge of blooming. It has three layers of nine petals each, arching outwards or curving inwards to recreate the blossoming, to symbolize the enlightening of the mind. Nine pools of water encircle the structure, and through them, nine walkways lead to nine entrances into the central prayer hall. A hall of silence and reflection. A reflection on peace.

Religious texts, mythology and folklore are very descriptive and replete with images of scenes, people and events. Naturally, they also mention a mind-boggling variety of plants, trees, herbs, flowers, weeds, grasses, groves and forests. Some of these have specific roles or are linked to deities, and are thereby sacred; others exist simply as metaphors or for aesthetic value. Let us read about a few of these.

DIVINE DARAKHT: HOLY TREES OF ISLAM

In the Quran, the holy book of Islam, and the Hadiths, sayings of Prophet Muhammad ﷺ, nearly 100 plants are named. Some are figs, olives, grapes, bottle gourds, corn, barley, tamarisk, ginger, camphor, saffron, senna, fenugreek, cucumber, aloe, marjoram, black cumin, chicory, cress and the toothbrush tree or miswak.

About the pomegranate, a Hadith recorded by medieval scholar Abu Nu'aim says that there is no pomegranate that does not possess at least a single seed from the pomegranates of Jannah, or the garden of paradise. As for abundant shade-giving acacia, it was a reward from Allah for true followers. It sprouted like an oasis in the desert, offering shelter from the sun. The date palm, valued for its nutritious fruit and useful foliage, is mentioned the most. The Prophet ﷺ is believed to have said: 'Whoever says: 'Glory is to Allah, the Magnificent, and with His Praise (*Subhan Allahil-Azim, Wa Bihamdihi*)', for him a date palm is planted in Paradise.'

The Ayat an-Nur or 'Verse of Light' in the Quran, says:

Allah is the Light of the heavens and the earth. His light is like a niche in which there is a lamp, the lamp is in a crystal, the crystal is like a shining star, lit from the oil of a blessed olive tree, located neither to the east nor the west, whose oil would almost glow, even without being touched by fire. Light upon light! Allah guides whoever He wills to His light. And Allah sets forth parables for humanity. For Allah is All-Knower.

Note the phrase 'located neither to the east nor the west'. A tree located to the east would receive sunrays only in the morning; to the west, only in the afternoon. But this is no ordinary tree. Due to its ideal location, it is bathed by nourishing sunlight all day, which is why its luscious fruit gives excellent oil, clear and pure like liquid gold, glowing like the *nur* of Allah.

At a practical level, the Hadiths teach us that trees are signs of Allah, and reveal the wisdom in His creation. We must offer thanks for these gifts that make our life on Earth not only possible but also worthwhile. We should care for trees, plant more of them and maintain them to demonstrate faith. There are also references to seeds, grains, pollination, cultivars and genetics, thus referring to important concepts like biodiversity in non-scientific terms.

The Prophet often uses trees as similes: 'The believer who recites the Quran is like the citron, which tastes and smells good. The believer who does not read the Quran is like the date, which tastes good but has no smell. The hypocrite who reads the Quran is like the sweet basil, which smells good but tastes bitter. And the hypocrite who does not read the Quran is like the bitter

apple or Zaqqum, which tastes bitter and has no smell.' Okay then, who's up for some personalized perfume?

But beware the Zaqqum! When the kings of Saba (called Sheba in the Bible), a wealthy, spice-trading kingdom, did not appreciate the wonderful weather Allah sent their way (so that they could build dams, roads and gardens), but instead worshipped the sun, they faced a destructive flood that destroyed all their fruit-giving trees and left only the Zaqqum with its utterly pungent fruit, as bitter as the heads of serpents. It is the tree that grows in hell, and its fruit is the only food available to those who refuse to believe in Allah.

If there's a Hell Tree, there must be a Heaven Tree too, right? Indeed there is. In a Hadith, the Prophet ﷺ describes a wondrous tree to a Bedouin tribesman. Talking about Paradise, he says that there grows the Tuba tree, which is 100 years big. That's a strange description, don't you think? Remember how a light year is not a measure of time but of distance? Similarly, what this analogy implies is that the tree's shadow is so immense that a rider would have to travel for 100 years to cross it. The girth of its trunk is so colossal that a sturdy desert camel would probably collapse due to old age and exhaustion before it could go around it even once. Its boughs are laden with gigantic bunches of grapes. Each bunch measures the distance a crow can fly non-stop in a month. And dare we ask how big one grape is. Well, big enough to feed an entire Bedouin tribe. Whoa, that sounds like a divine lesson in mathematics.

BIBLICAL BOWERS:
FLORA FROM CHRISTIAN LORE

Who hasn't heard of Adam, Eve and the apple? Like other scriptures, the Bible too is replete with ecological metaphors. It is said that Christ peppered his parables with imagery of plants, trees, fruit and the gigantic glories within small seeds. In fact, let's begin with his parable of the mustard seed, which appears often across the gospels of Matthew, Mark and Luke.

Describing the kingdom of God, Jesus said: 'It is like a mustard seed. It is the smallest of all seeds on Earth yet when sown, it grows up and becomes larger than all garden plants and puts out large branches, so that the birds of the air can make nests in its shade.'

Well, we know that there are seeds smaller than the mustard, and that the mustard does not become a tree—but let's focus on the essence of the fable. The point is that the origin of the kingdom is tiny, almost insignificant: just Jesus, his apostles and some followers. But slowly, in fertile soil (receptive minds) and with regular nutrition (faithful followers), it spreads its branches and shelters all people (birds), not just the chosen Jews and steadily flourishes across the globe. The seed reveals its colossal core. The growth of Christ's church confirms his parable, his gospel.

Back to the apple, a fruit found in lore galore: from Greek myth (golden apples gifted by Gaia to Hera and Zeus) to Norse legend (apples of immortality guarded by Iduna) to Grimm's fairy tales (poisoned red apple that made Beauty *sleeeeeep*) and more. This may be so because many old languages use their word for apple to refer to all fruit! (Quite like Steve Jobs would have wanted the Apple logo to be on all computers in the world.)

In the Old Testament, Adam and Eve lived in paradise, innocently happy in their birthday suits, till the smooth-talking serpent (aka the Devil) tempted them to eat the forbidden fruit from the tree of knowledge. In one bite, they knew joy, and then shame. After all, they were wearing, well, nothing. When God saw them, he knew that they knew. For this disobedience, he banished them from Paradise to Earth, which they had to populate. That's the Fall of Man. Incidentally in early Christian art, the fruit shown for this episode is a fig. You see, the Bible does not actually mention an apple. Possibly the shift happened later due to mistranslation or wordplay as in Latin, apple is *malus* and evil is *malum*. And so, the apple came to symbolize many things: immortality, temptation, knowledge, sin.

The concept of original sin—a result of this big fall—holds that all descendants of Adam and Eve, that is, all of us humans, are born into sin. How does this connect with the tree of knowledge, which could well be seen as the 'tree' or the cross in Golgotha, on which Jesus was crucified to save humankind from sin? If Adam was disobedient and sinned, Jesus is obedient and atones for that original sin, and all the sins here and evermore. So, the apple came to represent the overcoming of sin. You canst now sink thy teeth into that crunchy Honeycrisp thou hast in thine hands . . .

On the night before his Crucifixion, Jesus is said to have prayed in Gethsemane (from the Hebrew for 'oil press'), an olive grove with an oil press inside. Sadly, the imagery is of crushing and beating, like olives in a press, Jesus on the cross. As if Jesus

were God's olive tree and his grace or oil would be poured out to wash away all sins of all humans. It also suggests Christ's coronation as King, not just of Jews but all men.

In Biblical tradition, olives provide many things like food, fuel, medicine, anointing oil, sacrificial oil, cosmetics and wood for furniture, and symbolize many things from beauty, joy, honour and productivity to Israel and the Holy Spirit itself. And lest we forget, peace and hope. *The Book of Genesis* tells us that when the Great Flood was ebbing, Noah sent out a dove to check whether it was safe for the ark's creatures to emerge. The dove returned with 'a plucked olive leaf in its beak'. The olive was the first to be reborn, giving hope to all. It was time for new life to sprout. The olive branch has been a symbol of renewal and peace ever since.

KRISHNA'S COMPANION, THE KADAMBA

Krishna, the playful god, is often called Muralidhar, Venugopal or some variation due to his linkage with the bamboo flute, *murali* or bansuri or *venu*. However, another tree was truly integral to his life and *leela* (divine deeds), as we know from the Bhagavata Purana and depictions in art, especially miniature paintings. In Vrindavan, it was in the scented shade of the Kadamba, with its globular, golden, butterball-like flowers that Krishna played his flute mellifluously, frolicked with his cowherd buddies and flirted with hundreds of gopis but most romantically with Radha of Barsana. It was from the Kadamba's branches that he suspended the skirts and veils of dozens of shocked-and-awed

gopis, who had dared to skinny-dip in a pond. Some call it a metaphor for how the human soul must shed all its 'clothing' of worldly knowledge and bare itself to god. Or it could simply be the mischief of a child.

But it was hardly a mere mischief-maker who clambered up the trunk of the lone Kadamba on an island in a part of the Yamuna where the evil naga Kaliya lived, seething, frothing, transferring toxins into the water for miles around. The tree was immortal because Garuda the eagle had spilt some amrit as he perched on it on his way back from the heavens. One day, when the gopas and cows drank the toxic water and collapsed, off the Kadamba's bough leaped valiant Krishna straight into the river. The enraged Kaliya coiled around him, but Krishna slipped out and jumped on to his hoods, where he danced. Each step of his landed like a thunderbolt, and the serpent slowly collapsed as Krishna stood yet again on the crown of the eternal Kadamba.

TREE OF LIFE, THE PEEPUL

In the Bhagavad Gita, Krishna declares: *Vrikshanam ashwathoham / Ashwattha pujitoyatra pujita sarva devta* ('Among trees, I am Ashwattha / To worship the Ashwattha is to worship all gods'). It is believed that Krishna lay under a peepul tree, when a hunter's arrow caused his passing from mortality back to Vaikuntha. Legend also says that the tree is Trimurti itself: the roots are Brahma, the trunk Vishnu, the leaves Shiva. Even in Harappan seals and pottery, the peepul tree motif occurs frequently, suggesting that it was venerated and also loved from an arty point of view. In Sanskrit, the name can be split as *a-shwa-ttha*, where *a* means 'not', *shwa* means 'tomorrow', and *tha* means 'that which still stands'. So Ashwattha could mean 'one that does not stay the same tomorrow'. Just like the universe, which is always transforming.

In this shaping-shifting world, there was one stable spot: under the chosen peepul, the Mahabodhi (*bodh* meaning 'knowledge'), where Siddhartha the bodhisattva transformed from seeker to enlightened, the Buddha. Buddhists believe that at the exact moment when Siddhartha was born in Lumbini, this tree sprouted spontaneously about three *gavutas* or 4 km (as per the *Pali Tripitaka*) from Bodh Gaya. This was *Prithvinabhi*, Earth's navel, where all began. This tree of nirvana was the birth site not only of the Buddha, but Buddhism itself. Pilgrims from across the world travel great distances to the Mahabodhi, which is their Mecca, their Jerusalem. In the third century BCE, in his bid to spread Buddhism, Emperor Ashoka sent, among other relics, this tree's sapling to the ancient city of Anuradhapura (called Anurogramma by Ptolemy). There, it still flourishes as Jaya Sri Maha Bodhi, a 2000-plus-years-old symbol of divinity.

Can you solve these clues to find the missing tree names?

1. Tree worshipped on Vat Purnima in memory of the death-defying love of Savitri for Satyavan

2. Tree that propped Trishanku up between Earth and heaven; its fruit bears Shiva's *trinetra*!

3. Sacred herb, avatar of Lakshmi, ceremonially married to Vishnu to mark the end of monsoon

BRINGER OF FORTUNE, THE BEL

The *Shiva Purana* calls it 'the symbol of Shiva'. The *Skanda Purana* tells us how it took root when Parvati's sweat rolled down from Kailash to Mandara. As a prank, she blindfolded Shiva with her palms, but then the whole world went black! So Shiva opened his third eye for a bit, its fiery heat made her sweat, and that's how the bel or *bilva* came to be. With a new tree around, and not a bad looker, she made it her holiday home. It is believed that Parvati lives in its roots as Girija, in its trunk as Maheshwari, in its branches as Dakshayani, in its fruits as Katyayani and in its flowers as Gauri—no wonder Shiva adores it.

Offering the trifoliate leaf, *belpatra*, to Shiva is particularly beneficial. Its three leaflets perfectly echo the image of Shiva's trident, his potent trinetra and his triad of worldly chores: create, preserve, destroy. Naturally, people believe that offering these cosmic-customized leaves can cancel out negative karma of their three previous births! The *Shanti Parva* of the Mahabharata recounts the tale of the hunter Suswara. Stranded in a dark, deep forest once, he spent the night perched atop a bilva. Forlorn without his family and warm home, he cried. Fearful of wild animals, he chanted Shiva's name. To keep awake, he plucked and dropped leaves to the ground. Morning came, sun shone, he reached home and forgot all about that night . . . till he died and went to heaven. There he found out how his luck had turned because he had

In Jainism, Shitalanatha, the tenth Jina or tirthankara, is said to have attained Kevala Gyan or complete understanding (nirvana) under a bilva tree.

unwittingly worshipped a Shiva linga under that tree. His tears had cleansed it, his chants had resounded in it and the leaves had covered it in devout piety.

TAKER OF SORROWS, THE ASHOKA

In his fifth-century romcom *Malavikagnimitram*, the poet Kalidasa praises the scarlet splendour of the Ashoka's bloom, even likening its flowering and fruiting to childbirth; it literally does not blossom till a maiden kicks it! The tree is known well from the Ramayana, in which the kidnapped Sita rejects Ravana's opulent palace and opts to live in Ashoka Vatika, the grove where Hanuman finally finds her. They say she could bear her *shoka* ('sorrow') at being parted from Rama only because she was surrounded by *a-shoka* ('without sorrow') trees, which she admired during her *vanvas* for the way the leaves emerged copper-coloured—hence the name Tamraparni—and slowly took on enchanting hues of green. Not only a grief healer, it is also called Premvriksha (tree of love), and its fragrant blossoms form the tip of one of Kamadeva's love-inducing arrows.

From the *Bhavishya Purana* comes an older fable. A prequel to the tale of Sita Ashok, in fact. A cannibal called Sashoka preyed on humans in the Dandakaranya forest, killing and devouring with relish, without pity. One day, he was struck by the serenity on the face of a meditating sage. He had never seen such peace, let alone experienced it. He wanted it too, there and then. Well, it clearly wasn't the age of Amazon Prime same-day delivery, so he had to wait. Quite a bit. If he lived a life of prayer and penance, said the rishi, he would one day be reborn as a tree in Lanka. You know the one: sheltering Sita, harbouring Hanuman. The ex-man-eater promptly agreed. And since Sashoka would one day catalyse the end of Sita's sorrows, the sage dropped the S for sorrow and renamed him Ashoka.

Nature spirits and guardian deities called yakshinis in Buddhist, Jain and Hindu mythologies are often depicted along with flowering Ashoka trees.

Can you solve these clues to find the missing tree names?

1. Garlands of this fragrant white flower, symbolic of selfless devotion, are offered to Hanuman

2. Seeds that rolled down Shiva's face as he blinked after meditating open-eyed for a thousand years

3. Tree whose blossom forms the fragrant tip of the most potent arrow in Kamadeva's quiver

If this chapter has planted curiosity in your minds, go forth and explore. There are so many more divine trees across myths and legends. Observe, listen, read and you could come up with your own book! For now, to test your eco IQ, here is a fun crossword on legendary flora.

CLUES

1. Also called gopher wood, the tree Noah used to make the legendary ark before the Great Flood (7)

2. Symbolic flower of Ahura Mazda; used to represent the oneness of God in Nowruz ceremonies (6)

3. Tree sacred to the Bishnois; it is said the Pandavas hid their weapons in it during their one year of incognito exile (7)

4. (Across) The form God took to appear to Moses on Mount Horeb (or Sinai); take a hint from the answer to #5 (7,4)

   (Down) Sacred bundle of twigs, often taken from pomegranate trees, used in Zoroastrian religious ceremonies (8)

5. In the parable of Jotham from the Torah, the berry-giving shrub that finally agrees to rule over all trees (7)

6. Sturdy tree, the wood of which was used by Solomon the Wise to build the First Temple of Jerusalem (5)

7. 'Lady of the forest', local protector deity worshipped by both Muslims and Hindus of the Sundarbans (7)

8. Goddess Parvati's avatar with which the chinar tree, locally called *bouin*, is closely linked in Kashmir (7)

9. Mythical herb needed to revive the comatose Lakshmana; to get it, Hanuman uprooted Dronagiri peak (10)

10. Hyssop, on a stalk of which a vinegared sponge was offered to Christ on the cross, is said to be this plant (8)

11. Intensely aromatic flower that Shiva cursed; not used in worship but essential to cosmetics and cooking (6)

8

TIMELESS TOMES

Epics from the Cultures of the Land

Every culture has its magnum opuses, the blockbusters that people remember for generations. In the old days, these epics were recited as stories and passed down from generation to generation (getting altered down the line, a bit like Chinese whispers). Every faith has its scriptures, also passed down the ages, which contain ideas, thoughts and philosophies behind the faiths and their deities. Together, they make for a fascinating bit of reading and a great way to understand peoples and their cultures.

Here's a fun activity, the WordWorm! You must decipher the clues to find the name of an epic, a scripture or an associated element. Fill the word in the correct segment of the worm. See the worm breaking out of the shell, right in the centre? That's where you begin. The first letter of the first word is revealed already. Then you simply go round and round, anticlockwise, filling up the creepy-crawly. Big hint: the last letter of every word is the first letter of the next.

CLUES

1. These are the earliest scriptural works in the Hindu tradition, which one Hayagriva stole and another Hayagriva recovered! The word literally means 'knowledge'. (5)

2. These scriptures are said to be discourses of the Buddha himself. Short or long, they get their name from the Sanskrit word for 'thread'. (6)

3. This is a kind of composition by Jain monk-scholar Bhadrabahu, credited with spreading the philosophy to south India (as per the Digambaras) and Nepal (as per the Swetambaras). (7)

4. This was the very first compilation of the Sikh holy book, done by Guru Arjan Dev in 1604 and installed in Darbar Sahib. (3, 6)

5. These oral and written traditions are believed to describe the words and actions of Prophet Muhammad ﷺ, as laid down in the Quran. (6)

6. In Vedic ceremonies, different priests specialized in different texts and had different roles to play. This one was the priest of the Rig Veda. (5)

7. This book, which is believed to have been given to Prophet Isa by Allah, is sometimes referred to as the Gospel of Jesus. (5)

8. This is an epithet often used for Moses, on account of his bringing to his people the Commandments and giving them the rules by which to live. (8)

9. This last book of the New Testament (and thus the Christian Bible) is known as the *Apocalypse of John* and foretells Christ's second coming. (10)

10. Written by Acharya Kundakunda and called *The Perfect Law*, this Jain text explains the path to liberation by practising austerity and right thoughts. (9)

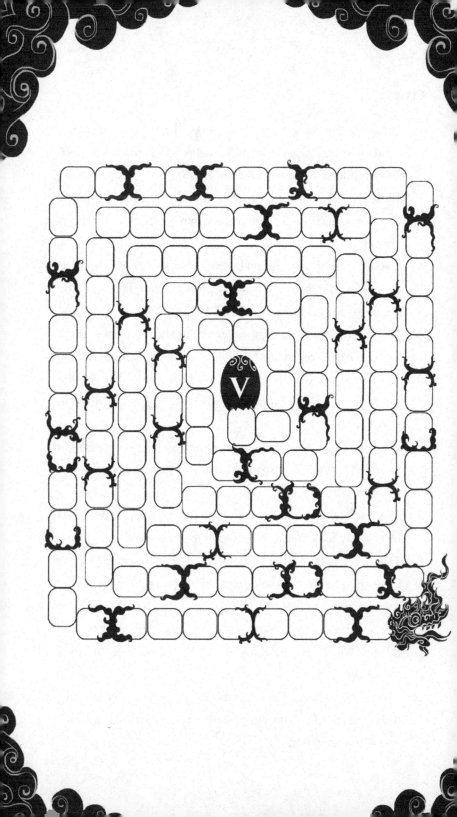

11. This is the Parsi holy book, whose primary part or *yasna* (named for the ceremony of worship) comprises Gathas composed by Zoroaster himself. (6)

12. These ancient texts explain Buddhist principles in a way that is easy to understand, by using simple, direct language and avoiding any interpretation by authors. (10)

13. This is the practice of asking for one's sins to be forgiven, and Yom Kippur, the Jews' holiest day, is set aside for it. (9)

14. Also known as the Pali canon, this is a collection of the basic teachings, lessons and philosophies of Buddhism. (Hint: The Pali word, not Sanskrit.) (8)

15. This type of Vedic text describes rituals, their underlying philosophy and elements such as mantras, myths and symbols; named for the term for 'wilderness'. (8)

16. This is the Semitic language in the classical form of which the holy Quran has been written and must be recited. (6)

17. This is the dynasty during whose reign the Thevaram anthology of verses praising Shiva (which are said to have catalysed the Bhakti movement) was collated. (5)

18. These were Jesus's followers, whose interpretations of his life and teachings form the New Testament. The word originates from the Greek for 'messenger'. (8)

19. This is the foremost and oldest Digambara text. Since the original Jain scriptures were lost shortly after Mahavira's nirvana, this document is highly regarded. (13)

20. This fourth Veda, very different from the first three, was not considered a Veda earlier and is sometimes called the 'Veda of magical formulas'. (7)

9

CALL OF DEITY: LEGENDARY WARFARE

Arguments, Conflicts, Battles and Wars

What's a good myth without a grand battle? Conflicts between gods and anti-gods have forever symbolized the tussle between good and evil. You may know of the Mahabharata and Ramayana wars, in which the Pandavas battled the Kauravas, and Rama's multicultural armies took on Ravana's. But that's just the tip of the iceberg. Legendary folk—men or women, gods or demons—loved to fight. If they didn't have enemies to confront, they would take on each other!

The Tarakamaya Sangram was a fascinating face-off, devas against devas, until the asuras couldn't resist and joined in too. It all began with Soma (or Chandra, the moon god) being too handsome for his own good, and Tara, the wife of Brihaspati (guru of the devas), not being able to resist his charm. *Uh-oh.* Brihaspati couldn't tolerate his wife running off, so he attacked Soma. Now, Shukra (guru of the asuras) was always at odds with Brihaspati, so he immediately took up arms for Soma. Seeing this, Indra and Rudra sided with their outnumbered guru. The asuras joined Soma while the devas united with their leader Indra. There was utter confusion and massive destruction of the created worlds. Brahma, the Creator, was aghast that all his hard work was being undone, so he managed to bring both squabbling sides to the negotiation table. Tara was sent back to Brihaspati, but Soma held on to Budha, the son they had together. This is mentioned in the Puranas as one of the twelve *kolaahals* or battles fought primarily by the devas.

THE BATTLE BEGINS

Though many texts would have us think so, it wasn't just wives and sisters that drove people to war. For instance, in those worlds, if you were rude to someone, it could lead to unforeseen consequences—as Indra found out to his dismay aeons ago. Tvashtri, one of the personifications of Vishwakarma, had a son named Trisiras, or 'the three-headed'. Now, Indra was insecure and thought that this multifaceted (literally!) personality could prove to be a threat to his position as the king of gods and so,

he killed him. Problem solved. But wait . . . An enraged Tvashtri created a terrible demon called Vritra, with the sole purpose of killing Indra. Sometimes called a serpent, sometimes a dragon, Vritra is the personification of drought and thus, the exact opposite of Indra, god of rain. Indra and Vritra fought battle after battle, until the gods had to intervene (yep, that does happen a lot) and broker a truce. According to the terms of the peace treaty, Indra could not attempt to kill Vritra with any weapon made of metal, wood or stone, either by day or night. So how did Indra get around these clauses? Quite the strategist, he fought Vritra at twilight—the time *between* day and night, neither one nor the other. For his weapon, he used sea foam—not metal, not stone, not wood. Infused with the power of Vishnu, this fatal foam was what finally overwhelmed the demon.

There is another version of this rivalry. One day, busy admiring himself in the way many selfie-takers tend to, Indra managed to royally ignore Brihaspati. Miffed and insulted, the preceptor simply disappeared. As a result, the guru-less devas started getting defeated by the asuras in every conflict. Brahma advised them to request Trisiras, yes that three-headed dude, to become their guru until Brihaspati returned. The agreement was on and the devas' faith in themselves was restored, leading to increased success in their skirmishes with the asuras. However, Indra found out that while conducting sacrifices for the devas, Trisiras—who was an asura on his mother's side—was also slyly placing offerings on their behalf. Flying into a rage, he beheaded the brand-new guru. This enraged his dad Tvashtri, who created Vritra—the demonic powerhouse of fire and heat—to vanquish Indra. War resumed, and now it was the devas' turn to lose. And yet again they ran to Brahma, who

guided them to ask sage Dadheechi for his bones (ouch!) and use them to craft a highly potent weapon. Thus came about the famous vajra, Indra's prized weapon, with which he finally killed Vritra. Before he died, Vritra would keep reminding Indra that he had committed Brahmanahatya, having decap-*cap-cap-*itated Trisiras. So even though he won this battle, Indra was so overcome with guilt that he fled Swarga and hid where no one could find him.

You can find out where he went in 'A Leaf of Faith', page 139.

BEASTLY TALES

Indra's slaying of the dragon Vritra is echoed in Christian legend, where St George (the patron saint of over a dozen countries and cities, most notably England) is famous for having slain a dragon that demanded—and received—human sacrifices that he relished. Although he is reliably recorded as a real person, the son of a Roman named Gerontius in the third century CE, George is said to have fought in the First Crusade, which is impossible because the Crusades began almost 800 years after his death. In any case, the tale for which he is legendary is set in Libya, where a dragon had terrorized the locals, demanding first sheep and goats, and then humans, to satisfy his insatiable hunger. When it was the turn of the king's daughter to be gobbled, up popped George jabbing his trusty lance named Ascalon to slay the evil dragon and rescue the princess. The overjoyed and grateful king gave George gold and jewels, which he distributed among the poor, thus earning the people's respect and ensuring their baptism in the new faith.

In Hindu mythology, Kaushika was a powerful king of Kanyakubja. During a hunt in the forest, he and his companions reached Vasishtha's hermitage. Exhausted and hungry, they gladly took up the sage's invitation of rest and refreshment. A smorgasbord of a feast was conjured up by Nandini, who was the talented daughter of Kamadhenu, the original wish-fulfilling divine bovine. This magical calf was Indra's gift to Vasishtha, so when Kaushika asked for it, the sage flatly refused. After all, parting with it would have seriously increased the ashram's living expenses! When the angered monarch sent his soldiers to capture her, she produced an entire army to defeat them. Not one to give up, the king returned with his *sena*, which could easily defeat a mere Brahmin. Vasishtha, however, deployed his ascetic powers to rout the army of Kanyakubja. Finally realizing that he needed help, Kaushika prayed to Shiva and managed to get some divine weapons in return. Armed with these, he killed Vasishtha's 1000 sons, but then out came the old man and vanquished Kaushika, again. His Brahmanic powers simply absorbed everything that Kaushika hurled at him. Back went the king to greater penance, along the way creating new mantras, including Gayatri, the most powerful of them all. Slowly, he realized that all that he was praying for was worthless compared to the spiritual power that penance gave him. He became a great sage and was renamed Vishwamitra, or 'friend of the world'. Their rivalry remained, however.

WORLD OF WARCRAFT

In Hindu mythology, the biggest and baddest battle was the Mahabharata or the great war of Kurukshetra between the cousins, Pandavas and Kauravas. Almost everyone in the land (and outer lands) was part of this battle, which very few survived. However, before this war, there was another colossal clash: the Battle of the Ten Kings. As the story unfolds in the Rig Veda, there was an ambitious king called Sudas, who wanted to expand his kingdom. Guided by his guru Vasishtha, he set about becoming the region's Chakravarti, or overlord. The kings of the neighbouring areas were obviously not happy with Sudas's expansionist policies, and so they banded together against him. These clans—Alina, Anu, Bhalana, Bhrigu, Druhyu, Matsya, Pani, Parsu, Puru—faced off against the armies of Sudas near the river Iravati (now Ravi). The fierce battle raged on for days, months, even years, some believe. Finally, it seemed that Sudas had had enough, for he retreated across the river. His enemies weren't going to let him go, however, and followed him. And then, as if by divine intervention (have you learnt about deus ex machina yet?), there was a flash flood. *Drip-drizzle-splash-bloooooop* . . . The force of the water knocked out most of the pursuing army and Sudas seized the opportunity to turn around and hammer the final nail in their coffin! The hurly-burly of the battle was done, and Sudas became Chakravarti. By some accounts, this meant that the Vedic Aryans extended their reign over all of north India. Other scholars interpret this as a clash between Vasishtha and Vishwamitra all over again, though they

are not agreed on which of the two sages was Sudas's preceptor, and which one was against him.

Some battles are fought to cause death and destruction. Some are fought to prevent mayhem. Like the next one we will recreate. You would remember how Vishnu took on the avatar of Narasimha, half-man half-lion, to kill Hiranyakashipu and save Prahlada. Well, N's divine energy was not dissipated even after accomplishing this mammoth task, so he went on a rampage, slaying and slaughtering everything and anything that came in his way. The frightened devas (when were they not, actually?) propitiated Shiva to help them get Vishnu's angry avatar off their backs. Happy to help, the lord of Kailash decided to bring out his inner beast. To challenge the man-lion, he transformed into Sharabha—described in various texts as part-lion, part-eagle or an eight-legged deer with violent tendencies or a thirty-armed bird with as many weapons. The two fought on, with neither getting the upper hoof until Vishnu decided to change his form, again. This time, he opted for the form of Gandaberunda, a superstrong, two-headed mega eagle that could carry off mighty elephants in its talons. As soon as he switched to this avatar, his Narasimha fever subsided, as he realized his work was done and he could return to Vaikuntha. So did Shiva, back to Kailash.

FEMMES FATALES

When there are endless tales of males (gods, demons, men) engaging in battle after battle, it is difficult to imagine that the females would stay behind. However, it appears that the demon Mahishasura was not that imaginative. He thought he was invincible because of a boon from Brahma. *Who else?* He had wished that no man, deva, *yaksha*, *gandharva* or asura could ever defeat him. Thus unchallenged, he swiftly conquered the mortal realms and approached Devaloka. The terrified gods went to Brahma, Vishnu and Shiva, who used the gender loophole in the boon contract. Sadly for Mahisha, there was no Girl Up then, and in his male-dominated thought process, he never imagined that a female could actually be more than a match for him. All the gods then concentrated and their collective inner shaktis emerged in the form of the many-armed Durga.

Each god then gave her a weapon of choice so that her many hands would be put to good use. From the divine vahana pool, she chose the lion and rode off to battle the demon for days, matching

Read more about Durga's weapons in 'Heavenly Hardware, Bulletproof Beings', page 189.

him blow for blow while he shifted shapes to escape. For nine days and nine nights, they duelled. Finally, as he was transitioning into his original mahisha (buffalo) form, Durga struck through his defences with her trident and killed him. The nine days of battle are now commemorated as Durga Puja Navaratri, while the tenth day is celebrated as Vijayadashami.

If you thought that Shakti, the female power, was only invoked once to finish off Mahishasura, think again. Not much later, up rose the demon siblings Shumbha and Nishumbha, who defeated the devas, occupied their heavenly domains and thus challenged the world order. These bothersome brothers also had a boon from Brahma that no male could kill them. Clearly, they did not know, or believe, that history repeats itself.

The homeless gods turned to the Trinity for help and, yet again, the shaktis were called to action. In came the awe-inspiring, lion-riding Ambika. Um, perhaps the daitya duo was just a bit wary of this feisty female who came to engage with them without fear, because they first sent in their hordes led by fearsome asuras Chanda and Munda, with bows bent and swords drawn. Seeing them so eager to fight catalysed some darker power within Ambika. She knitted her eyebrows and from her forehead sprang out Kali, wearing tiger skin

 and a garland of human skulls, carrying the scary, skull-topped club called Khatvanga, and basically looking like death itself. Chanda and Munda stood no chance and soon lost their skulls. And this is how the goddess also came to be known as Chamundi. Since delaying the inevitable doesn't prevent it, finally Shumbha and Nishumbha went into battle themselves. Sure enough, they too met their end at the hands of Ambika.

A Bollywood-level side episode in this battle of the sexes was the combat between the goddess and another asura Raktabeeja, also a henchdemon of S and N. Now this guy's boon (received

from Shiva) was that whenever a drop of his blood touched the ground, a clone of his would come alive there and then. So no matter how many times Durga, Ambika or the other shaktis killed him, his blood kept creating even more clones. (Those among you who are Star Wars fans are probably imagining them as the Stormtroopers!) Once again, Kali was summoned to counter this maya and she spun her dark magic, capturing and drinking every drop of blood that spilled, *before* it could touch the ground. As the input stream dried up, so did the production of Asuratroopers, and the rest were wiped out one by one.

SIBLING RIVALRY

Fights among brothers have been part of our common histories forever. Cousins went to war and we had the Mahabharata. But did you know about the bickering brothers in the Jain tradition? Legend has it that Bahubali, also worshipped as Gomateshwara, was one of the 100 sons of Rishabhanatha. After their father gave up his throne and retired to a life of penance as the first tirthankara, his eldest son Bharata took charge of the kingdom of Ayodhya. He decided to conduct a yagna to become a Chakravarti, the most powerful king in the world. At his command, the Chakraratna or golden wheel with spikes went rolling across the lands and wherever it passed, kings would either submit to his supremacy and pay tribute, or wage war and be defeated by the armies accompanying it. The wheel came to a halt by itself at the kingdom of his brothers. (Dad's realm had been divided 50:50 between the eldest and the rest of his offspring. Unfair, much?) Now, ninety-eight of the brothers willingly paid tribute, but Bahubali refused and challenged bade bhaiyya.

Interestingly, the confrontation between Bahubali and Bharata was held in three formats: eye war, water war and fist war. Bahubali easily won the first two rounds, defeating big brother in the stare-till-you-blink (or giggle) eye combat and then the water fight (hmm, wonder how they went about this one), and was getting ready for the third when he suddenly had an epiphany and realized the error of his ways. Disgust overcame him and he gave up his riches and kingdom to become an ascetic. A peaceful end to a peaceful battle, in classic Jain tradition.

As in other faiths, in Parsi mythology too, there is a constant tussle between the forces of good and the troops of evil. The forces of good, like knowledge, benevolence, light and life itself, represented by Ahura Mazda and the Spenta Mainyu, combat the Angra Mainyu, or Ahriman, that symbolize darkness, ignorance, death and all the other negativity known to humans. In Avestan Zoroastrianism, the battlefield can be physical (this world) as well as metaphysical (the minds of humans). The struggle between good and evil exists all the time, inside us and outside us, right up to the final showdown when good will finally triumph over evil, when Judgement Day for all souls will arrive, when the world will be destroyed to be rebuilt anew.

CHAIN OF COMMAND

Given the countless wars and battles described in Hindu scriptures, you would expect an infinite number of warriors too. And you would be right. But who is the greatest of them all? As sports fans would wonder, who's the GOAT? Here's a dekko at various levels of battlers, but do take their numbers with a generous helping of salt. At the basic level, the bottom of the pyramid, is your normal everyday soldier. They don't count for much, except as a statistic for higher levels.

A **RATHI** is a highly capable warrior, mounted on a chariot and capable of fighting 5000 regular foot soldiers simultaneously. Some known rathis are Nakula, Sahadeva, Yudhishthira, Shikhandi and all the Kauravas.

An **ATIRATHI** is a level higher than and capable of taking on twelve rathis, or 60,000 foot soldiers at the same time—*wow*! Some known atirathis are Bhima, Drupada, Vibhishana, Jambavan, Satyaki, Jarasandha, Shalya and Pradyumna.

A **MAHARATHI** equals twelve atirathis, or 144 rathis, which means he can take on 7,20,000 soldiers in battle. That equals half of the Indian Army active today. Imagine that

one Maharathi, skilled in weaponry and combat, could possibly defeat them all. Some known Maharathis are Parashurama, Arjuna, Bhishma, Drona, Kripacharya, Abhimanyu, Karna, Angada, Kumbhakarna, Sugriva and Lakshmana.

An **ATIMAHARATHI** is the next grade of warrior who equals twelve Maharathis (calculate how many soldiers that implies) and be confident of coming out alive. He is almost the apex predator of the classical Hindu Puranic jungle, adept at all weapons, including most divine ones, and capable of destroying all enemy formations. Some known Atimaharathis are Rama, Krishna, Indrajit, Hanuman and Shiva's avatar of Bhairava. (And the number you are looking for is 86,40,000 soldiers.)

A **MAHA-MAHARATHI** is the top of the heap, the GOAT. Indeed, the Maha-maharathis are the greatest of all time among warriors, and can do basically anything they want. They up the scales, being able to fight twenty-four Atimaharathis simultaneously or 20,73,60,000 ordinary soldiers (told you, they are good only as statistics) and are just about invincible. And who are these gods of combat? Literally the super-gods. Some known Maha-maharathis are Vishnu, Shiva, Brahma, Ganesha, Kartikeya and Shakti (Durga, Ambika, Chandi, Parvati, Lakshmi, Saraswati, Kali . . . any form of the goddess).

THE BUDDHA VERSUS MARA:
A BATTLE IN THE MIND

Buddhism is a faith focused on ahimsa but not without its good versus evil battle between Mara and the Buddha. More than a battle, it is a cold war. Mara is the lord of death, the king of fantasy, the embodiment of vices like greed and hate, the personification of the dark side of human nature, the evil one. To depict his power, Mara is often shown as a warlord atop an elephant, with millions of troops at his command. When translated in Pali and Sanskrit, Mara means 'killer'. In a discourse, the Buddha said that no power is 'so hard to conquer as the power of Mara'. What is astonishing is that Mara attacks neither with warriors nor weapons but with temptation. He gets into your mind. He makes you desire things, leaves you dissatisfied and unhappy. He makes you hungry, thirsty, restless, fearful. He makes you ambitious yet lethargic. He brings out the worst in you.

Though Mara tempted the Buddha often, their greatest showdown happened under the Bodhi Tree, as Gautama meditated to attain moksha. Mara sent many distractions his way, including his daughters Trishna (thirst), Rati (desire) and Raga (delight), to break his focus. Epic fail! Then he sent a raging storm of rain and rock, ash and darkness to blur his vision, cloud his understanding, divert him from his goal, but Gautama was unmoved. As the 'arrows' of temptations neared

Gautama, they lost their sharp anger, turned into flowers and fell around him like offerings. The Buddha said: 'Mara, I will destroy your army with the power of wisdom, just as an unfired pot is smashed by a stone.' Mara's final challenge was a question: 'Who do you think you are? How can you claim the right to Buddhahood?' Gautama said nothing, just reached out to touch the earth with his hand, the *bhumisparsha mudra*. As if asking creation itself to support him and bear witness to his right to the final awakening. The earth shook and split, swallowing Mara's massive armies. *Gulp!* And back went Gautama into his trance, soon to emerge as the Enlightened One.

Mara vanished into the earth but did not stay long. He would pop up now and then to tempt the Buddha. And the Buddha would say: 'I see you, Mara.' Instead of driving away the evil one, he would offer Mara a cushion to sit on and a cup of tea. Mara would sulk awhile and leave, his evil intent quashed yet again. And the Buddha would smile.

DEADLY DESIGNS: BATTLE FORMATIONS

When one is talking of battles, one also has to understand the tactics of battle. What weapons did people use? How did they prepare for war? Arjuna needed Krishna to give him 'Gita ka gyan' before he could lift his bow and fire an arrow at his own great-grand-uncle Bhishma or his guru Dronacharya. As for the armies, they were arranged in strategic formations, which would cause the most damage to the enemy but protect one's own soldiers. Perhaps the most famed formation is the Mahabharata's Chakravyuha, now synonymous with a situation that is impossible to get out of.

On the right are illustrations of some fascinating battle formations. Can you match them to the names on the left?

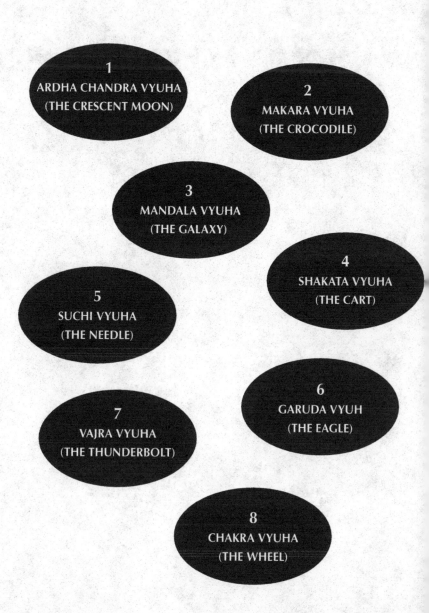

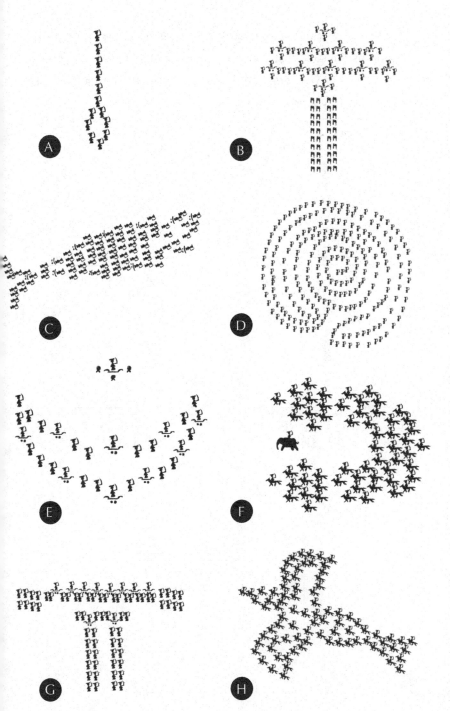

And here are the very interesting names of a few more army patterns. Imagine that you are a Maha-maharathi with countless troops under your command. Can you draw the formations you would send your soldiers out in?

OORMI VYUHA
(THE OCEAN)

KURMA VYUHA
(THE TURTLE)

TRISHULA VYUHA
(THE TRIDENT)

KRAUNCHA VYUHA
(THE HERON)

SRINGATAKA VYUHA
(THE HORNS)

CHANDRAKALA VYUHA
(THE CURVED BLADE)

MALA VYUHA
(THE GARLAND)

10

HEAVENLY HARDWARE, BULLETPROOF BEINGS

Almighty Weapons of Mighty Mythological Characters

Ballistic missiles, nuclear warheads, fly-by-wire weapon systems, anti-missile defence systems, diamantine—nay adamantine—armour . . . Do these sound like twenty-second century technologies? What if we told you that all these terms refer to legends of yore? Unbelievable, isn't it? Our collective mythology is a veritable arsenal of weapons that could ravage entire armies, rain down fire and vaporize oceans.

Across all mythologies and faiths of India, there were and are many, many deities—crores of them really, even if we count only the Hindu pantheon! Most of these gods and goddesses possessed fabulously fantastic weapons. Divine bows that were unbreakable and came complete with inexhaustible quivers of arrows; spears, tridents and maces that struck terror into opponents; arrows that hurled fire, water, snakes or mountains at the enemy; missiles that reduced entire armies to nothingness; and, the most spectacular of all, Sudarshana Chakra, the divine discus of Vishnu, considered the greatest weapon in all of creation because it was unstoppable, and unbearable, by any but its master.

Such legendary weapons were wielded not only by the gods but also by men and anti-gods. Like several other warriors of legend, Arjuna and Karna in the Mahabharata and Rama, Lakshmana, Ravana and Meghnad in the Ramayana could summon and deploy divine weapons after performing penance and undertaking extreme austerities to please the gods to whom all these arms or *astras* originally belonged. To summon these, they also needed special mantras, which their gurus or gods taught them.

KURVED FOR KOMBAT

We can safely say that the most extensively utilized weapon in Indian mythology is the bow-and-arrow combo, also called *dhanush-baan* or *teer-kamaan*. Mortals, demigods, gods and goddesses all deployed this curved asset of attack, some like

Arjuna and Eklavya with legendary dexterity. You probably also know about the jaw-dropping manner in which Rama strung and shattered Shiva's bow, which the strongest and boldest of warriors could barely budge, let alone lift. Let's check out some other fabled, fabulous bows.

Once, they say, sage Kanva (in whose ashram Shakuntala grew up) was so engrossed in his austere meditation that he didn't even realize when a termite-filled mound of earth arose around him and a bamboo sprouted from his head. Such immovable meditation! Promptly, Brahma appeared to grant him boons and, as a bonus, also transmuted Kanva's body to gold. Since the bamboo growing from Kanva's head would have unique qualities, he offered it to the divine architect Vishwakarma, who split it three ways to fashion this trinity of terrible bows.

PINAKA: According to some legends, Vishwakarma crafted Pinaka for Shiva to destroy the triple city of Tripura, set up by the three sons of the demon Taraka and populated by evil citizens. Some say Shiva fashioned it himself, using the mountain Mandara as its body and the serpent Vasuki as its string. Now such a marvellous bow would have had an equally amazing arrow, right? Curiously enough, Shiva shot just one arrow to destroy all three floating cities simultaneously, and this arrow had Vishnu as its shaft, Vayu as its two wings, Yama as its tail feathers and Agni as its arrowhead. (Psst, a little later we'll tell you more about this alarmingly accurate arrow that was shot from Pinaka.)

Meanwhile, let us remind you that though Pinaka was celestial, it was not unbreakable. During Sita's swayamvara, Rama not only lifted it—something none of the other kings and princes in attendance could manage to—but, in fact, also managed to shatter it as he was attempting to string it! So strident was the sound of its breaking that Parashurama heard it and came racing to Mithila to challenge this young upstart who had dared to disrespect the gods. To test Rama, the incensed ascetic brought out the next bow we are going to talk about.

But before that, take a moment to reflect on the enormity of this encounter. Parashurama and Rama, the sixth and seventh avatars of Vishnu, meet in the same physical dimension, face to face!

Read more about this in 'Gods of All Things', page 30.

SHARANGA (OR KODANDA OR VAISHNAVAT): So back to the highway between Mithila and Ayodhya, to the once-in-forever showdown between the two avatars. Parashurama confronts Rama: if you can manipulate one bow, surely another one is not too much of an ask? And he promptly produces the magnificent Sharanga, the bow of Vishnu, the proto-avatar. He challenges Rama to use Sharanga and duel with him. Rama bows respectfully and, as he is bowing, he snatches the bow in a jiffy, strings it, draws an arrow and points it straight at P's heart . . . challenge accepted! In the same instant, P realizes that he is face to face with, well, himself. He does the only reasonable thing to do and presents Sharanga to Rama, who goes on to use it for a lifetime of battling evil and eventually takes it back with him to Vaikuntha.

Earlier, Vishnu had presented it to sage Richika, who gave it to his son Jamadagni, who gave it to his son Parashurama. Later, in Dwapar Yuga, Sharanga reappeared on Earth when the avatar Krishna offered it to Arjuna during the Mahabharata war.

 DEADLY DISCUS

Saranya-Sanjana, wife of Surya, could not bear his brilliance, so her father Vishwakarma shaved off some of Surya's shine! With the solar particles, he crafted three objects: Pushpak Vimana, Shiva's trishul and Sudarshana Chakra. In some Vishnu temples, the chakra is worshipped as a person along with his consort Vijayavalli.

GANDIVA: It is said that Gandiva was as massive as a palm tree and its 108 unbreakable strings rumbled like thunder when plucked, striking dread in the enemy. It was resplendent, covered with golden discs that reflected the light that hit it, briefly blinding onlookers. When it launched arrows, it glowed so intensely that none could look at it. Gandiva could fire hundreds of arrows over hundreds of miles, defeating lakhs of opponents as it amplified a normal arrow's potency a thousand times. What's more, it came with two quivers of inexhaustible arrows. One could try to count the arrows but would simply end up counting forever, as they would forever keep replacing themselves! Some versions say that Brahma himself forged Gandiva from the heavenly tree Gandi and used it for a millennium before it passed on to Prajapati, Indra, Chandra, Varuna and Agni and finally reached Arjuna. Agni gave Gandiva to Arjuna so that he would keep Indra occupied. As a result, Indra would not be able to rain out Agni's efforts to consume Khandava forest. When he wielded it, Arjuna was truly invincible. Others who could use it were Krishna, Bhima, Karna, Bhishma and Parashurama.

VIJAYA: Now what would mythology be without a dash of mystery? It seems that the only bow in the Mahabharata war that could match Arjuna's Gandiva was Vijaya, literally 'victory'. Who do you think deserved it? Karna, of course! And how did Karna come to possess this bow that originally belonged to none other than Shiva? It is believed that Shiva had entrusted Indra to hand it over to Parashurama for his mission of eliminating all the Kshatriyas of the world. That done, the militant sage then gave the bow to Karna, his favourite disciple, who armed with it would probably have defeated Arjuna on the penultimate day of the war but for a snag in his chariot and some not-so-righteous manipulations by Krishna.

In other accounts, Vijaya was just another name for Pinaka. Well, that's how myths work.

BOW DOWN, MISTER!

Quite different from this assemblage of destroyers was the bow of Kamadeva, god of love and beauty. This amazing 'weapon' was made of stalks of sugarcane with a line of humming bees and beetles as its bowstring. It fired arrows tipped with five fragrant flowers: white lotus (*aravinda*), blue lotus (*nilotpala*), jasmine (*navamalika*), Ashoka and mango. He also possessed five other arrows, named Unmadana, Tapana, Sosana, Stambhana and Sammohana, for the effect they would have on the victim. Guess what Kama, or Manmatha (he who stirred the mind of Brahma), conquered with those arrows? (Hint: He was Hindu myth's Cupid.)

THE GEAR OF A GODDESS

A bow was just one of the 'wowsome' weapons that a goddess like Durga would wield, given that she had 4–18 arms! Once this feisty deity was manifested, she needed arms and ammunition. Her fellow gods gifted her some cool gizmos to defeat the demon

Read all about the origin of Durga in 'Call of Deity: Legendary Warfare', page 170.

Mahishasura: bow or *dhanush* (from Vayu) and arrows or *teer* (from Surya), together symbolizing her control over all energy sources; thunderbolt or vajra (from Indra, for focus in battle); disc or chakra (from Vishnu, for overcoming the life–death cycle); sword or *khadaga* (from Mahakaal, for strength and wisdom); trident or *trishul* (from Shiva, for elimination of all miseries—physical, mental, spiritual); elephant goad or *ankush* (also from Indra, for swift and decisive action); axe or *parashu* (from Vishwakarma, for the destruction of ignorance). She also had in her kitty Shakti the spear and a mace from Agni, Pasha the noose from Yama, Khitaka the club from Kubera, and the conch or shankha as well as Nagapasha the missile from Varuna. This last weapon could spout venomous snakes . . . Not someone you'd like to go up against, eh?

ASTRAS, THE SURPRISE ELEMENTS

You already know that the gods had really cool powers up their sleeves and would dish these out to other gods, demigods and

humans as and when the need arose. Or when they felt like it! Apart from the (relatively) commonplace Agneyastra, which rained fire on whoever it was hurled at, and the similar Varunastra and Vayavastra, which poured water and blew stormy winds, the Brahmastra had the power of Brahma himself and could pierce any armour, however impenetrable. This terribly destructive weapon was used by Kaushika (later known as Vishwamitra) against Vasishtha. The latter coolly absorbed its power with his staff, the Brahmadandastra, a weapon imbued with the power of the saptarishis and capable of being used offensively as well as defensively! The Brahmastra was also the weapon Lakshmana used to kill Ravana's son Atikaya.

If you thought this was powerful, it had a further evolved form called the Brahmashirshastra, which was powered by Brahma's four heads. It destroyed anything that came in its path and unleashed terrible flames, thousands of falling meteors, unbearable noises and horrific tremors across the earth. Wherever it struck, nothing would grow for twelve years. And it wouldn't rain either. All metal, all earth would be poisoned. Sounds like a modern-day H-bomb. The Brahmandastra, with Lord Brahma's five heads as its tip, was a super-super-weapon even further along the evolution ladder. If used, it could boil off all the oceans and vaporize all creation without leaving any trace, not even ashes. Some say it was created by the saptarishis to counter any weapon of any god.

Yet another deadly astra was the three-forked Pashupatastra, which contained all the power of Shiva, who used it to destroy Tripura, the triple city of the asuras. Do you remember which bow he drew it with? Now let's see how accurate it was. The

celestial cosmopolis, which comprised three different cities floating around on three different platforms at three different heights, was impossible to destroy because all three parts had to be hit simultaneously with the same weapon. Shiva waited for a thousand years for them to line up—must have paid attention in geometry class!—and in that split second, released the Pashupatastra. *Kaboom!* Arjuna received this fearsome astra from Shiva after an intense physical combat with Mahesha, who had taken the form of a Kirata (hunter) to test him. Arjuna used it to kill Jayadratha, whom he blamed for the death of his son Abhimanyu.

Then there was the Narayanastra, one of Vishnu's personal weapons. When invoked, it would fire millions of deadly missiles. The only way to save oneself was to submit to it completely. Ashwatthama invoked it against the Pandavas, but Krishna ordered all the soldiers to drop their weapons, thus saving the army. Krishna came to Arjuna's rescue on another occasion when Bhagadatta deployed the deadly Vaishnavastra. Keshava simply stood up in front of his cousin and absorbed the weapon, which turned into a garland of flowers on meeting its creator. Since the greatest warriors were taking part in this greatest of wars, it was obvious that the greatest of weapons would be used too. Drona too used the Sammohanastra, which could cause people to fall into a trance, to stupefy Yudhishthira and capture him, but Sahadeva foiled his plan.

Karna had obtained the Shakti Astra from Indra in exchange for giving up his impenetrable *kavacha* (armour). Ironically, Karna wanted to use it to kill Indra's son Arjuna, but he was forced to target Bhima's son Ghatotkacha instead, giving up the single-use arrow. He tried (unsuccessfully) with a Nagastra, tipped with a

venomous snake that wanted revenge against Arjuna for wiping out his clan in the great fire that consumed the Khandava forest. Arjuna, in turn, used his dad's decapitating weapon Anjalikastra to behead Karna while he was stuck: literally, as his chariot wheel had sunk into mud, and figuratively, as a curse by Parashurama had robbed him of the knowledge of weapons at the moment he needed them the most.

Also present but not used in the Kurukshetra battlefield were the Tvashtarastra, which baffled the soldiers of an army such that they mistook their comrades for their enemies and started killing them, and the Mohini Astra that dispelled maya. Barbareeka's three arrows, which he received from Shiva according to some sources, also formed a fascinating firearm. This son of Ghatotkacha, unbeatable in war, would always fight for the underdog. The problem was that whichever side he took would promptly become stronger, so after killing off a few of his opponents, he would switch sides and join them. This process would continue till everyone apart from him was dead! Krishna figured that this scenario didn't fit into his own plans, so he knocked off the boy. But not before Barbareeka had demonstrated his three divine arrows. When shot, the first would mark all that was to be destroyed, the second would identify all that was to be spared and the third would actually finish the work. Another amazing weapon was the Raudrastra, which created a three-headed being with nine eyes in the sky, wielding a trident and raining down creatures like lions, tigers, bears, buffaloes, serpents, *sarabhas*, *chamaras*, *garudas*, *yakshas*, elephants, bulls and boars upon the enemy from the sky. And you thought it was bad enough when it rained cats and dogs!

MARTIAL MONKS

Okay, enough of this armed anarchy. Let's see what else we have . . . Wouldn't you agree that Buddhism is considered to be the world's most peaceful religion? And yet, it has its own demons and evil forces that must be defeated, at times through the use of force. One of the main weapons depicted in Buddhist iconography is the five-pronged vajra, a style of club with a ribbed spherical head. The four prongs at each end curve around the central fifth to form the shape of a lotus bud. You may spot (though rarely) a nine-pronged vajra in Buddhist art. Meaning 'thunderbolt' as well as 'diamond' in Sanskrit, the vajra is a very powerful weapon, used by bodhisattvas like Vajrapani (who even gets his name from it) to defend Shakyamuni (Gautama Buddha) from any demons trying to harm him. Like the one originally wielded by Hindu rain god Indra, the diamantine vajra destroys all but is itself indestructible. So overlapping and overwhelming are Indian myths that, in fact, Vajrapani was identified with Indra by fifth century CE scholar Buddhaghosha.

Another interesting cosmic accessory in the hands of a Buddhist deity is the *khagga* (or khadaga) gracefully held aloft by Manjushri. Gentle by name this bodhisattva may be, but he is the lord of intense wisdom, and his flaming sword of awareness is more a weapon of the mind or intellect, a weapon he uses to cut through the cobwebs of ignorance, of delusion. As such, it is a weapon of great symbolic importance for a Buddhist on the personal journey towards self-awareness and, eventually, enlightenment.

If Manjushri is gentle and wields a metaphysical weapon, at the other end of the spectrum would be the wrathful Padmasambhava—he who resurrected Buddhism in Tibet and subdued the other malevolent gods that had appeared to distort and destroy the way of the Buddha's teachings. This fearsome deity wields his hybrid trident-like trishul khatvanga, the three sharp points of which stand for essence, nature and compassionate energy, and the three skulls (one fresh, one rotting, one dried) adorning which represent the three bodies of the Buddha: *dharmakaya, sambhogakaya, nirmanakaya*. The weapon is embellished with hair from dead and living *mamos* and *dakinis* (angry female deities who can cause environmental disasters if humans disturb the elements), a sign that Padmasambhava managed to control them, through his severe austerities. Interestingly, the trishul is also used to represent the Buddhist triratna (Three Jewels: the Buddha, the Dhamma, the Sangha) and is often seen on stupas, coins and Buddha footprint relics. Perfect balance of war and peace?

 MOON'S SMILE

After defeating Kubera and commandeering his Pushpak, Ravana was gallivanting about when he was blocked by Kailash, Shiva's abode. Ravana tried to uproot the mountain, but Shiva pressed his toe and crushed him! Cleverly, he started singing paeans to Shiva, who released him and gifted him the powerful, crescent sword Chandrahasa.

THREE-POINT STRATEGY

Quite a striking weapon to look at, one you would also associate with powerful Graeco-Roman deities like Poseidon and Neptune, the trident is popular in Indian iconography as trishul and perhaps most closely identified with Shiva. Some legends say that it was with his trishul that Shiva decapitated Ganesha. And it was the very same trishul that Shiva presented to Durga. Its three blades are said to denote the three fundamental aspects of life: *ida* and *pingala*, the outer ones, represent the duality of Shiva and Shakti, or masculine and feminine; while *sushumna*, the central one, represents the still state of undisturbed bliss.

Like most things mythological, the trident too is interpreted variously. Some believe it is not just to be equated with Shiva, but indeed with the triumvirate of Brahma, Vishnu and Shiva, for it iconizes the trinity's functions of creating, preserving and destroying. Speaking of destruction, it is also believed that the trishul can destroy all three worlds: this world of ours, the world that belonged to our forefathers (our heritage) and the world we can only imagine.

And since we love the symbolism behind numbers, here are some more interesting interpretations. The trident's three prongs could stand for any or many of these: the Tridevis (Lakshmi, Saraswati, Kali); the *gunas* (*tamas, sattva, rajas*); the three lokas (bhu, Swarga, Patala); body, mind, atman; clarity, knowledge, wisdom; death, ascension, resurrection; and—of course—past, present and future.

CROSSFIRE CROSSWORD

Pick up your weapon, aka your pencil, and crack this crossword to discover new weapons.

CLUES

1. Bow created by Brahma, given to Arjuna by Agni, and returned to him after the Kurukshetra war (7)

2. When hit by this mind-bending astra, warriors of the same army would mistake each other for enemies and begin to fight amongst themselves! (8)

3. Terrible weapon that poisoned the earth such that nothing could grow for twelve years (13)

4. Snake weapon used by Meghnad to bind Rama and Lakshmana (9)

5. Vishnu's weapon, which destroyed all opponents, sparing only those who submitted to it (12)

6. Shiva's divine sword, the one he gave to Ravana, was named thus for its crescent shape (11)

7. Also called Subrahmanya and Skanda, the wielder of the weapon known as the Vel; given to him by his mother (9)

8. (Across) The great bow of Shiva, now a deadly weapon in the arsenal of the Indian Army! (6)

   (Down) The great arrow or astra of Shiva and Kali, which can be used only to uphold dharma (9)

9. Indra's powerful weapon, which Karna used to kill Ghatotkacha (6)

10. Sage who willingly gave up his life and donated his bones so that the omnipotent vajra could be fashioned (9)

11. Created by Vishwakarma out of 'sun dust', this was the legendary disc of Vishnu with 108 serrated edges (10)

GUESS THE WEAPON

1. You never see Hanuman without it or, for that matter, Bhima. Ganesha prefers it too and Vishnu's even has a name: Kaumodaki. Duryodhana was convinced it was the greatest weapon of all and we are sure Jarasandha agreed. What is it?

   _____

2. Vishnu is, at times, shown brandishing one called Nandaka. Ali ibn Abi Talib had a scissor-like, double-blade one called Zulfiqar. In Parsi legend, it appears as Shamshir-e Zomorrodnegar, the only weapon that could kill the horned demon Fulad-zereh. What is it? _____

3. Balarama taught both Bhima and Duryodhana the art of fighting with the _gada_, but his own preferred weapon was something quite unique. Owing to his association with this equipment, possibly named Samvartaka, he is also called Halayudha or Halabhrit. What is it? _____

4. Kartikeya's Vel, presented by Parvati, was instrumental in vanquishing the asura Soorapadman. It represents wisdom via its long shaft (years of learning), broad face (number of books to be read) and pointed tip (analysis of what has been read). What is it? _____

Here are some legendary warriors and their favourite weapons.
Can you identify and label them, and then match the pairs?

1 _____   _____ A

2 _____   _____ B

3 _____   _____ C

4 _____   _____ D

11

IN THE NAME
OF THE FATHER

Problematic Paters from the Legends

There have been some unbelievably bad dads across world mythologies, and Indian mythology is no exception. You know what they say about family, right? You don't really have a choice in the matter. Though, after reading this chapter, you will probably realize exactly how lucky you are to have the family you have. There are some terribly mean dads in legend, and they pop up across mythologies. You may have read about Kronos, the Greek Titan who swallowed his own children Hera, Hades, Poseidon . . . till his son Zeus (cunningly saved by mum Rhea) forced him to, well, vomit out his siblings. Here, we bring you just a few Indian dads: mad, bad, rad!

SHIVA AND GANESHA

Shiva is known for his anger and raging but once he went totally ballistic and chopped off his own son's head! Well, to be fair, he didn't know at the time that Ganesha was his son. According to the *Shiva Purana*, while Shiva was away on one of his jaunts, Parvati fashioned a child's statue with clay and—*poof*—breathed life into it. It was this loyal kiddo standing sentinel outside his mum's bath the day Shiva decided to return home. Ganesha would simply not budge and give way to the lord, because mummy had said so! Sages cajoled him, deities pleaded, but he stood his ground. That's when Shiva lost it and lopped off Ganesha's head. You can imagine the scene when Parvati finally emerged—by the way, how could she not hear the hullabaloo?—and would only be consoled by Shiva bringing their dead son back to life. Wait, no, Parvati got really, really angry at Shiva's impetuous antic, and sent forth her Shaktis to basically destroy all the gods. When Brahma, Vishnu and Shiva tried to placate her, she would have none of it. All she wanted was her son, alive. So Vishnu chopped off the head of the first living creature they saw and Brahma glued it on to the headless body, and gave it life. And that's how Ganesha got his pachyderm pate and is worshipped as the elephant god. Quite a beastly tale that!

HIRANYAKASHIPU AND PRAHLADA

Made pretty much invincible by a boon from Brahma, demon king Hiranyakashipu had conquered all three worlds and driven out the gods from the heavens. He was not a believer but his son Prahlada was forever praying to Lord Vishnu. Now, Hiranyakashipu hated Vishnu's

You would have read about this in 'Gods of All Things', page 17.

guts because Vishnu in his Varaha incarnation had killed off his brother Hiranyaksha. He took it all out on his own son. He sent fearful demons, toxic serpents and mighty elephants to attack Prahlada, but all that the boy had to do to protect himself was think about Vishnu. Nothing whatsoever could harm him— neither poisoned food nor hallucinations created by the demon Shambarasura. Holika, his aunt who was immune to fire, tried to burn him alive by seating him on her lap inside a bonfire. Instead, she got roasted! And this is why a symbolic 'Holika' or pile of wood is burnt with much rejoicing the night before Holi. Ultimately, Vishnu had to take on his fourth avatar of Narasimha, half-man and half-lion, to kill horrid H at twilight on the threshold of his glittering crystal palace. Must say our myths have a thing for dramatic irony!

ARJUNA AND ARAVAN

And now, coming to the Pandavas. They were valiant warriors, obedient sons and loyal brothers but devoted dads . . . let's see. The Naga princess Ulupi was one of the four wives of Arjuna. They didn't live together much because Draupadi, the main wife of *all* the Pandavas, would have none of it. So shortly after, Arjuna left Ulupi and their son Aravan (also known as Iravan or Iravat), who grew up to be a formidable warrior and found his way to Lord Indra in heaven. What's the connect? Well, Indra was his granddad after all, being Arjuna's biological dad. Anyway, news of Aravan's skills, not the least of which was his being well-versed

in maya (skills of illusion), spread and Arjuna (without any guilt whatsoever) asked him to fight on the side of the Pandavas in the ubiquitous Great War. On the battlefield, with the help of his ferocious serpent army, Aravan overpowered many warriors, including the demon-reincarnate Srutayush; Vinda and Anuvinda, princes of Avanti; and a slew of siblings of the wily Uncle Shakuni of the Kauravas—till he was decapitated by the mega rakshasa Alambusha, who had transformed into a garuda or eagle-man, arch-rival of snakes. Poor thing!

HEAD OVER HEELS

Aravan also 'lost his head' in *Parata Venpa*, an early Tamil version of the Mahabharata, but in a different manner. During the war, when the Kauravas gained an upper hand and a sacrifice to Kali was the only way to ensure a Pandava victory, Aravan offered himself. For this selflessness, Krishna granted him the boon that his cut-off head would 'see' the war through to the end. It symbolizes the end (death) as well as the continuity (sight after death). In some temples in south India, you can actually see just Aravan's head being worshipped. Does it not make you think about what good a war is when innocents suffer the most?

By the way, his head got Aravan into trouble in the afterlife too! In the post-war gossip session, the Pandavas were gloating about their victories. Since Aravan had witnessed it all, Krishna asked him: 'Who has truly been responsible for this victory?' Promptly, Aravan said: 'Well, I remember two things:

Krishna's chakra decapitating the enemies and Krishna's conch collecting the blood.' Uh-oh! That was not something Bhima wanted to hear from his nephew. So he lunged for the head, but Krishna was faster and dropped the head into the Caraparika river. In the water, the head became a child, who went on to kill the demon Kuttacuran. Thereafter, he got another name: Kuttantavar, slayer of Kuttacuran.

BHIMA AND GHATOTKACHA

After killing the demon Hidimba, Bhima the Pandava married his sister Hidimbi (also called Hidimbaa). However, he left soon after their son was born; because Hastinapura was calling! Ghatotkacha, his abandoned son, became a fearsome warrior. Tapping into his inner part-demon, he could fly, turn invisible and become huge or tiny. His grandmother Kunti had made Hidimbi, promise that G would turn up whenever the Pandavas needed him. Ponder a bit over the unfairness: he had no father to nurture him, but he could be commandeered to play his father's saviour whenever, wherever. So, of course, he was recruited for the Big War. He defeated great warriors like Ashwatthama and Duryodhana, killed the mighty demons Alambala and Alayudha and was poised to finish off the war on his own. The Kauravas pleaded with Karna to use his amazing Vasavi Shakti, which could

kill anyone that Karna willed it to. Now Karna had been saving it to destroy his arch-rival Arjuna because it could be used only once, after which it would return to its original owner, Lord Indra. The Kauravas convinced Karna that G was a greater danger, and he agreed. The Shakti pierced G's heart and he fell, but even as he fell, loyal son that he was, he expanded into a ginormous size and crushed thousands of Kaurava soldiers. What a sacrifice!

WAR OF THE WORLDS

What happens when two great warriors face off? When the mighty Ghatotkacha and the skilled Karna had a showdown, everyone watched. G flung a *chakrayudha* (discus) at K, who smashed it to smithereens with his arrows. Using his magical powers, G conjured up a mountain to project weapons, but K destroyed it with his thunderbolt, Vajra Astra. Then, G invoked a cloud that could rain down boulders, but K countered it with his wind weapon, Vayu Astra. G uprooted and hurled trees, K snapped them with arrows. G created many versions of himself, K fired off arrows at each one and G swallowed all the arrows! When this didn't seem to work, G shrank and shrank and shrank till he became invisible, and then shot forth weapons of fire. Ultimately, K had to pull out the Vasavi Shakti and bring down his opponent.

WHAT'S THE CONNEQT?

On the left are names of some fathers who managed to make legendary errors in parenting, and on the right are the names of some of these kids as well other kids of these fathers. Can you match the columns?

FATHERS	SONS
Bhima	Puru
Shiva	Bhishma
Arjuna	Sutasoma
Shantanu	Prahlada
Hiranyakashipu	Lava-Kusha
Uttanapada	Kartikeya
Rama	Abhimanyu
Yayati	Dhruva

12

FESTIVALS OF THE FARAWAY FOLK

A Look at Celestial Celebrations

Joy, sorrow. Prosperity, poverty. Birth, death. God, demon. These have been part of the story of humanity for millennia, commemorated and celebrated through festivals that have evolved over time. Every community honours its unique stories and characters through them. Let's look at the community camaraderie and religious rituals that festivals bring into our lives.

What do you imagine when you think 'festival'? There's Christmas, Hanukkah, Lohri, Holika Dahan, Diwali, Dussehra and many more. Visualize the elements of festivals. Is there a thread that connects them, like fire, food, plants, incense, chants? Festive fiestas often feature fire, as an *atar* or havan, as earthen or electric lamps, and as candles.

Food is another link. Feasting is an important part of the rituals, though the kind of food prepared and relished differs as per religious sanction. Rice, milk, jaggery, sugar, coconut, herbs, meats and dishes featuring these are crafted according to ancient traditions. In fact, during Pongal in Tamil Nadu, people usually greet each other, not by saying '*Vanakkam*' or '*Namaskaram*', but the rather cryptic 'Has the rice boiled?' Festivals are often dedicated to founders of faiths, prophets, saints and deities. Many incidents from their lives—such as birth, marriage, enlightenment, death, rebirth, victory—are preserved in legend and ceremony.

Here's a fun activity, another WordWorm! You need to solve the clues to find the name of a festival or something associated closely with it. Fill the word in the correct segment of the worm. See the worm breaking out of the shell, right in the centre? That's where you begin. The first letter of the first word is revealed already. Then you simply go round and round, clockwise, filling up the creepy-crawly. Big hint: the last letter of every word is the first letter of the next.

CLUES

1. This festival from Kerala celebrates the return of the ancient king Mahabali, or Maveli, from the underworld to his earthly abode. (4)

2. This is the day when Durga is said to have descended to Earth; Bengalis wake up early to recite hymns from the *Devi Mahatmaya*. (8)

3. On the birth anniversary of Mahavira, this ceremony is held to take out a procession of his idols and ritually anoint or bathe them. (8)

4. It is said that on Basant Panchami, this god of love disturbed Shiva's meditation and was blasted to ashes by the divine third eye. (8)

5. This is the food that devotees offer to the sun god on Chhatth Puja; it also refers to water-based offerings in rituals. (6)

6. Pongal is primarily a Tamil festival but is also celebrated in the neighbouring state of Kerala, where it is called _____ Pongala. (7)

7. This Buddhist festival of Ladakh and Tibet celebrates the arrival of the new year and spring with thanksgiving, merrymaking and feasting. (5)

8. The 'Lord of the Universe' and his siblings take this road trip annually, going from their own abode to that of Gundicha Devi. (4, 5)

9. This is the Chaturdashi, or last day of Ganesh Chaturthi celebrations, when the idols are taken out of devotees' homes and immersed. (5)

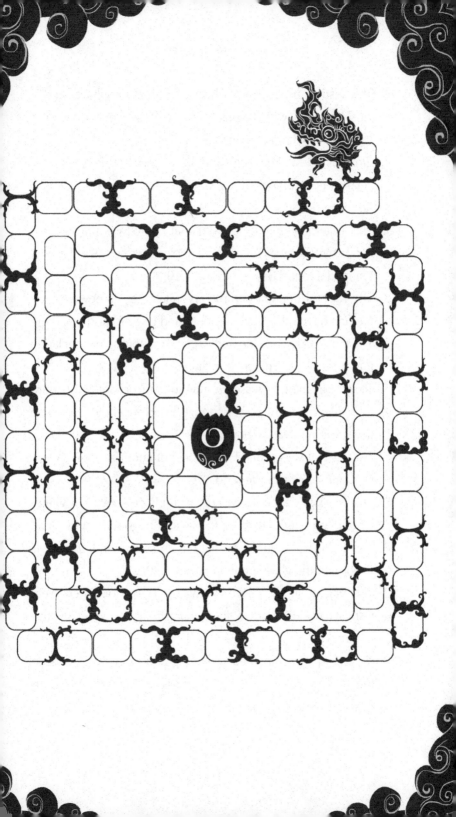

10. This festival marks the birthday of Padmasambhava, and is closely linked with Hemis Monastery, where the day sees spectacular Cham dancing. (6)

11. On this New Year celebration in Andhra Pradesh and Telangana, people wear new clothes, visit temples and feast on many flavours. (5)

12. This is another name for Mahabali, who was pushed into Patala by Vishnu as Vamana, an incident remembered as Bali Pratipada, four days after Diwali. (10)

13. The Kashmiri Pandit community celebrates its new year on the first day of the Chaitra month and gives it this name. (6)

14. The tenth Sikh guru decided to give Holi this name, declaring it as a festival to celebrate military prowess. (4, 7)

15. To kill Ravana on Dussehra, Rama had to chant this mantra to invoke the sun's power so that his arrow could overcome the amrit in Ravana's body. (14)

16. This festival sweet, filled with coconut and jaggery, is said to be Ganesha's favourite food. (5)

17. This masked dance festival of Sikkim is celebrated in winter by burning effigies to mark the victory of good over evil. (6)

18. This is the name given to that day in spring when the air is filled with the vibrant colours of Holi. (8)

19. The flag of Indra, raised during the auspicious New Year festival of Gudi Padwa in Maharashtra, is known by this name. (11)

20. Kshatriyas worship their weapons and craftsmen worship their tools on this day, which is a part of Navaratri celebrations. (5, 4)

Well done, you worked out the WordWorm! Now, you probably want to know more about these interesting festivals in the belly of the reptile. So here are some nuggets about each of the twenty festivals. But these are all jumbled now, and you need to match the festivals on the previous pages to the descriptions here. Once you've done that, fill in the letter circles with the correct word, and add the number that corresponds to the clue for the WordWorm. Get, set, go!

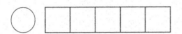

It is rooted in the customs of the older Bon religion that had a winter festival of incense burning, and this is now a fortnight-long celebration around the concepts of harvests and new beginnings. It is marked by festivity, like drinking of chhang and eating of khapse. The first three days, considered the most important, are dedicated to lamas, kings and deities, respectively.

Another new year. The previous evening, a large plate or *thaal* is filled with rice, on which are placed gold, silver, milk, curds, nuts, a pen, ink, an almanac, a picture of god, a mirror, sugar, flowers and bread. It is covered overnight and, in the morning, the family members view all the items, praying for knowledge, prosperity and divine blessings.

⬜⬜⬜⬜

In his Vamana avatar, Vishnu received a boon from Prahlada's grandson, a powerful asura. Vamana asked for three footsteps, assumed the gigantic Trivikrama form and started walking. Step 1: Earth. Step 2: Heaven. Step 3: Nowhere to go! So, the asura offered his head. Vishnu pushed him into Patala, his old kingdom, letting him return to Earth once a year on this day.

⬜⬜⬜⬜⬜⬜⬜⬜

Pujo celebrations in India have, for many years now, almost ritually begun with this programme, rousing and soothing all at once, being recited on radio by Birendra Krishna Bhadra. This is a radio show called 'Mahishasura Mardini', but has become synonymous with and famous as the day the goddess descended to Earth to fight Mahishasura and his demons.

⬜⬜⬜⬜⬜⬜⬜⬜⬜⬜⬜⬜⬜⬜

It seemed that Dashanana was immortal. Even divine weapons could not kill him. (Actually, the nectar of immortality in his navel gave him such power.) Finally, it was sage Agastya who taught the king of Ayodhya this way to summon Surya's strength. With his Brahmastra reinforced with solar power, the king could neutralize the nectar and kill the asura.

○ ☐☐☐☐☐☐☐☐

While Pongal is largely a festival of the Tamil region, the deeply shared cultural heritage with neighbouring Kerala has made way for a Guinness World Record. Every year, the _____ Bhagawathy temple in Thiruvananthapuram witnesses over 2.5 million women gathering for the _____ Pongala, the largest religious gathering of women in the world!

○ ☐☐☐☐☐☐

'Everlasting' is the meaning of the word. But what this 'chaturdashi' does end is the period of celebration of Ganesh Chaturthi, with a ritual *visarjan* or immersion, ten days after the idols are established with great fanfare in people's homes and public spaces. The 'remover of obstacles' takes away bad luck as he floats away on the waters.

○ ☐☐☐☐☐☐☐☐☐☐

Now, this gent here was one dynamic daitya and a benevolent ruler too. Like his grandpa, he was an ardent devotee of Vishnu, who incidentally had promised him that he would become the Indra of the next mahayuga. Of course, there was the small detour into the netherworld, courtesy a certain short-statured, umbrella-wielding, shape-shifting reincarnation!

On this ninth and final day of Navaratri, people across the land worship the instruments and implements that are meaningful in their lives. These could be ploughing and harvesting tools for farmers; carving, drawing, sculpting, weaving or painting tools for craftspeople; writing instruments for scholars; and weapons for soldiers. It is a day of giving thanks.

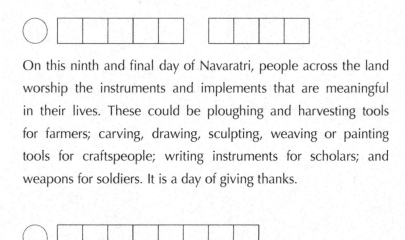

Abeer and gulal somewhere, rose petals and perfume elsewhere, sticks and stones too. This vibrant festival is a celebration of the eternal love of Krishna and his gopis, and also of the return of the god of love who, if you remember, was incinerated by Shiva. In Barsana near Vrindavan, women play a 'lath-maar' version, beating men with sticks. Tough love!

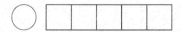

Once, when the asuras, led by Tarakasura, proved too much for Indra to handle, it was up to Shiva and Parvati to save the day. However, Shiva was in deep meditation, so Indra asked this Indian cupid to disturb the Adiyogi's penance. When he did so, a furious Shiva blasted him into a pile of ashes with his third eye!

Jagannatha, Balabhadra and Subhadra undertake this trip every year to meet the queen of Indradyumna, who is said to have built their home, their temple at Puri. They are dressed in finery and their chariots are pulled by thousands of devotees. The whole trip takes days, with stops at the grave of Salabeg (Jagannatha's Muslim devotee) and Mausi Maa temple.

When the final tirthankara of this age was born, it is said that the devas, led by none other than Indra, performed a ceremonial bathing of Mount Meru. To commemorate that, on his birth anniversary, his idols are ritually anointed and bathed by his followers, and then taken out in processions accompanied by the chanting of holy verses.

Yuga aadi—Sanskrit for the 'beginning of a new age'—is what marks the new year for the people of the home state of Kuchipudi. One of the key elements of the festival is the pachadi made with tamarind, neem flowers, jaggery, salt and mango (at times) to remind people that life is a mixed dish of diverse flavours.

○ ☐☐☐☐☐

The deity of good fortune had a great weakness for these sweet dumplings. Once, he ate so many that his large belly burst open and lots of them fell out. The moon couldn't stop laughing, and the skies echoed. Vinayaka lost his cool, broke off his tusk and hurled it at the moon, giving it a crater we can see even today!

○ ☐☐☐☐☐☐

People from Bihar, Jharkhand and eastern Uttar Pradesh set aside the sixth day after Diwali for their most important festival. The ceremonies, featuring ritual bathing, last four days. At the dusk of the third day and again at the dawn of the fourth, this main offering of food is made to the festival deity with prayers for health, wealth and happiness.

○ ☐☐☐☐ ☐☐☐☐☐☐

Guru Gobind Singh had to face the enmity of many, including the mighty Mughals. To unite his followers, he took an existing festival and added community participation in the form of religious sermons, singing and skill displays. From the initial gatherings at Anandpur Sahib, where it is still a huge attraction, the festival has spread across the world.

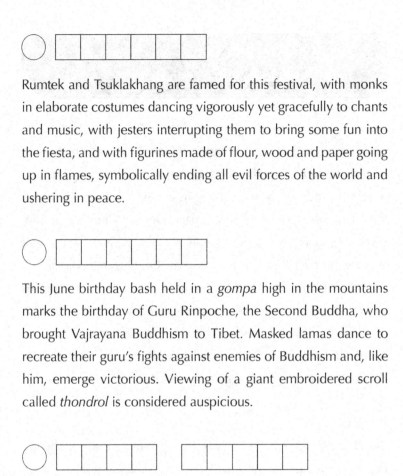

○ ☐☐☐☐☐☐

Rumtek and Tsuklakhang are famed for this festival, with monks in elaborate costumes dancing vigorously yet gracefully to chants and music, with jesters interrupting them to bring some fun into the fiesta, and with figurines made of flour, wood and paper going up in flames, symbolically ending all evil forces of the world and ushering in peace.

○ ☐☐☐☐☐☐

This June birthday bash held in a *gompa* high in the mountains marks the birthday of Guru Rinpoche, the Second Buddha, who brought Vajrayana Buddhism to Tibet. Masked lamas dance to recreate their guru's fights against enemies of Buddhism and, like him, emerge victorious. Viewing of a giant embroidered scroll called *thondrol* is considered auspicious.

○ ☐☐☐☐ ☐☐☐☐☐

This festival icon is a bamboo staff wrapped in colourful cloth, strung with flower garlands and topped with an upturned copper or silver pot. It reminds the god of rain to, well, make it rain. This auspicious day is celebrated as Sajibu Nongma Panba Cheiraoba in Manipur and as Cheti Chand by Sindhis.

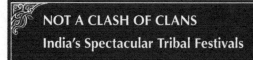

NOT A CLASH OF CLANS
India's Spectacular Tribal Festivals

Madai

This is an interesting 'mobile' festival of the Gonds of Chhattisgarh. It is celebrated to worship local deities of tribal populations and moves around central India. It begins in Bastar in December with the worship of Kesharpal Kesharpalin Devi or Cheri-Chher-Kin, then festivities move to other areas like Kanker, Narayanpur and Kondagaon over the next few months. On Shivaratri day in the month of Phagun (February–March), the ten-day finale begins in Dantewada, where village processions gather for dancing and singing. The Adivasis worship goddess Danteshwari in nine forms: Brahma-charini, Chandraghanta, Kumanda, Skandamata, Katyayani, Kalratri, Bhadragauri and Siddhidatri.

Bhagoria

The Bhils of Madhya Pradesh observe this spring festival. The fun begins a week before Holi, with melas and haats, or local village markets, springing up in parts of Jhabua and Dhar. Singing and dancing is the main entertainment, with a lot of the younger people using it as a platform to meet each other—social networking! The event culminates with the burning of the ceremonial fire that combusted Holika.

Karama

Another widespread tribal festival, this is celebrated across Jharkhand, Odisha, Madhya Pradesh, Chhattisgarh, West Bengal

and some parts of Assam too. An occasion to give thanks to the flora that sustains the tribes—a lot of different ones—this festival honours the karama (or kadamba) tree as a deity. Since the people are also cultivators, the event also lends itself to prayers for a good harvest. Nine types of grains are planted in baskets and looked after for nine days by young girls. Wonder what the boys are up to? Groups of people go into the forests and ritually cut branches of karama trees after praying to them, then bring these back to their villages and instal them in a central location for worship. Once the puja is over, the branches are immersed in the local river or stream, to again become one with nature.

Sume Gelirak

The Bonda tribals of Koraput region in Odisha are pretty reclusive. They don't interact with other people very much, probably because they were persecuted for centuries. They usually live simply but get together for this annual fiesta. Spread over ten days, the celebrations involve community singing, dancing and feasting, but the most striking part of the whole affair, literally, is the beating-up ceremony. Starting with little boys, then teenagers, young men and finally grown-ups, the males form two queues facing each other. Then, to the beat of the drum, they hit each other with tree branches. They have to grin and bear it, and the display of bravery continues till someone decides it's too much and gives up. They then touch each other's feet, embrace and go to get their wounds tended. This display of courage is probably intended to win the attention of a possible bride. Yes, that's what also happens in Sume Gelirak: young couples choose life partners for themselves.

Sammakka Saralamma Jatara

In Telangana, the Koyas celebrate what has now become the world's largest tribal festival, attended by over 10 million people every year. Dedicated to the mother-daughter duo of Sammakka and Saralamma, worshipped in the form of stick figures on the full moon (*pournami*) of Magha, this is an example of humans raised to divinity. Leading their tribe against the unjust rule of Kakatiya kings, Sammakka and her daughter Sarakka (later Saralamma) sacrificed their lives. (Shades of Boudicca against the Romans here?) People come in millions from across central and Peninsular India to offer jaggery and gold to the divine duo. In fact, it is the most attended religious event after the Kumbh Mela.

Dree

The Apatani tribe of Arunachal Pradesh celebrate this annual festival. They pay homage to Anw Donw and Abba Lwbo, legendary people who began cultivation in the fertile lands of Wpyo Supun, and overcame nature's challenges like storms, demons, insects and birds. This is echoed now in a series of rituals: Tamù, Metẁ, Medvr and Mepiñ. The Tamù is propitiated to ward off insects and pests, the Metẁ to avert epidemics and diseases that afflict humans. Medvr is a ritual to cleanse agricultural fields of unfavourable elements. And Dree concludes with Mepiñ, a plea to the gods to bless the crops. In modern Dree, people also pray to the Danyi for soil fertility, rich aquatic life in rice fields, healthy cattle and prosperity of all.

Pongto Kuh

In Tirap, also in Arunachal Pradesh, this 'wind-season time' is celebrated around April. It dates back to a time when animals,

trees and humans could talk to each other. Some Tutsa men once saw a group of monkeys playing a drum and dancing. They grabbed the drum and started imitating the monkeys. Since then, they have been doing it every year for this ten-day gala. They shift from village to village—dancing, worshipping produce like paddy, millets and fruit—and asking oracles how they can be happier and more prosperous.

AN ELEMENTAL ENERGY
India's Spirited Harvest Festivals

While these may not hold direct mythological relevance, still we cannot end this note on festivals without talking about the fun festivals, perhaps the most fun, linked to harvests and agriculture. From Lohri in the north with prayers and songs for good crops to the Punjabi Baisakhi, Himachali Minjar, Assamese Bihu, Malayali Vishu and Bengali Nobanno all to celebrate a good harvest, we Indians seize every opportunity to disrupt the humdrum of daily chores and just enjoy life. The north-east has Behdienkhlam, Wangala and K Pomblang Nongkrem in Meghalaya, to ask the old gods to bless the farmers and fields, and provide good, seasonal rains and bright sunshine so that the crops yield bountiful returns. Similarly, the Konyak, Ao and Angami tribes in Nagaland have their Aoleang, Moatsü and Sekrenyi celebrations with music, dance, feasting and offerings to gods and guardian deities.

The Koya tribals living in southern Odisha and northern Andhra have practised shifting cultivation for generations. In their main festival called Bijja Pandu, they worship Mother

Earth and ask her to bless their seeds (*bijja*) for a good harvest. Offerings of animals, eggs and fruit—mango plays an important role here—are placed before the goddess to make her happy. There is also a lot of singing, dancing, hunting and feasting in which everyone participates. The one thing that is not allowed is work. Wonder what happens to daily chores like cooking, cleaning, washing? In western Odisha, Nuakhai has farmers enjoying the fruits of their hard work in the paddy fields. They harvest, cook and feast on the new crop (*nua* is 'new', *khai* is 'food'), but only after they have offered the first portion in thanks to the gods. Here too, the celebrations are replete with community singing and energetic dancing.

Across the subcontinent, in Maharashtra, the Christian communities gather for Agera, perhaps the only Indian festival with a Latin-derived name; its root is the same as that of 'agriculture'. Earlier, locals of the region now called Mumbai celebrated it grandly but, with paddy fields giving way to urbanization, it diminished in size and importance. Determined not to lose this aspect of their culture, they still strive to preserve it. The festival begins with the priest blessing the field and symbolically harvesting a few stalks. These fresh-cut stalks are taken to church in a pretty palanquin, with the village band playing merry tunes. During Mass, the priest blesses these sheaves of the first harvest and distributes them among the people. When they return home, there is a festive family meal ending with a dessert made with the new rice.

FESTIVAL DIY

Here are some more festivals celebrated across India by its diverse, beautiful peoples. Why don't you find out more about these, and start a 'festiwiki' of your own. We will be happy to hear from you about celebrations specific to your community or region, as well as any that you think we should add to this chapter.

• Agni Keli	• Mitragan	• _____
• Ambubachi	• Nowruz	• _____
• Bani	• Pateti	• _____
• Baralu	• Pesach	• _____
• Bhai Dooj	• Raksha Bandhan	• _____
• Frawardigan	• Rosh Hashanah	• _____
• Gangaur	• Shivaratri	• _____
• Hanukkah	• Teej	• _____
• Id-ul-Zuha	• Thaipusam	• _____
• Jallikattu	• Thimithi	• _____
• Khordad Sal	• Tiragan	• _____
• Mim Kut	• Yom Kippur	• _____

13

THUGS OF HINDUSTAN

Demons and Anti-Gods

Do you wonder what gods and demigods in different mythologies would do if there were no evils to defeat or imbalances to fix? What would they protect and preserve if everything worked perfectly? Without ignorance, there would be little respect for knowledge. If no one lied or cheated, how would we learn what's wrong and what's right? Irritating and dangerous as they may be, demons and anti-gods complete the circle of creation, of life.

IN HINDU MYTHOLOGY

APASMARA was the demon of ignorance and nonsense speech, shown as a dwarf or a child to represent immaturity. (Though we strongly believe that children are the wiser ones!) Shiva assumed his Nataraja form to defeat him, but he realized that ending ignorance means undermining the effort to gain knowledge. *When in doubt, dance*, thought Shiva as he trapped Apasmara under one foot and broke into a joyful jig! Think about it: our inner demon can compel us to be rude to people, but we can control it by knowing better.

TATAKA, originally a yaksha princess with the strength of a thousand elephants, was cursed to turn into a rakshasi by sage Agastya because she, along with her sons Subahu and Maricha, would attack ashrams of sages and disrupt their prayers. So fearsome was she that not only men but even the clouds or sun avoided passing over the forest she lived in! Rama and Lakshmana were much braver, though, and killed her at the orders of their guru, Vishwamitra. (Some legends say she was Ravana's maternal grandmother.)

TARAKASURA, a diehard demon, repeatedly trounced the gods until heaven was about to collapse. He played smart and obtained a boon—from Shiva—that only a son of Shiva could defeat him. Pause for a moment here, relish the irony. He assumed that the ascetic Shiva would never have any children, but the gods

managed to get Parvati to marry Shiva. Then their son Kartikeya (or Subrahmanya) took out Tarakasura and defeated his brothers, Simhamukha and . . .

SOORAPADMAN, brother of Tarakasura, was about to be vanquished by Kartikeya when he transformed into a resplendent peacock and became his vahana. Earlier, he too had obtained a boon similar to his brother's and used it to raise Cain across Earth and heaven. During the ferocious fight with Kartikeya, he acknowledged defeat, begged forgiveness and was granted an avian avatar.

ANDHAKASURA emerged in the blink of an eye, literally. Once, Shiva was meditating and Parvati playfully covered his eyes, plunging the world into darkness, from which arose the sightless Andhaka. Shiva offered him to the asura Hiranyaksha, who was praying for a son. When A grew up, he performed penance and received a boon from (guess who?) Brahma that none but Shiva could kill him. Feeling invincible, A attacked and killed all and sundry, became a much-feared king and demanded to marry Parvati. Shiva refused, battle began and, for centuries, the two duelled until Shiva impaled A on his trident. Stuck there, realizing his folly, A started singing Shiva's praises until the god's heart melted. He forgave him, renamed him Bhringi and made him one of his chief ganas.

KALANEMI, Maricha's son and Ravana's cousin, had a mean mission: he had to prevent Hanuman from reaching Dronagiri to collect Sanjeevani, the herb needed to revive Lakshmana.

Kalanemi assumed the disguise of a sage, but the 'sage' simian saw through it, grabbed his feet, gave him a few good swings and hurled him right across to Lanka where he plummeted to his death. This story features in the *Adhyatma Ramayana*, a later version of the epic.

MADHU AND KAITABHA, the primordial asuras, are said to have been formed from—grossness alert—wax that oozed from a sleeping Vishnu's ears before creation began. They

promptly started praying to the gods, seeking invincibility. This time, the Devi obliged and when she did, M and K grabbed the Vedas from Brahma—as he was uttering them—and scooted off to Patala. Brahma roused Vishnu, who chased the miscreants and battled them for aeons. Unable to counter the boon, he tricked them by saying that he was pleased with them and would grant them another boon. Laughing their guts out, M and K reminded him that they were stronger and could offer *him* a boon instead. Then Vishnu asked them to kill each other . . . Uh-oh!

BHASMASURA, originally Brahmasura, is a classic case of a boon too soon. Pleased by his penance, Shiva granted him the boon that he could reduce any person to ashes, by placing his hand on their head. The asura promptly wanted to try it out . . . on Shiva! The panicking Pashupati ran to Vishnu, who assumed his Mohini form and entranced Bhasmasura, who now wanted to marry 'her'. The lady said she might, if he could prove that he danced as well as her. For days, crushing on her, Bhasmasura mimicked Mohini's moves . . . up until that graceful one ending with her hand on her head. Mirroring her, the besotted asura did the same and ended up a pile of ashes!

KRISH VERSUS KREATURES

*Young Krishna was targeted by a host of demons, several of them sent by his uncle Kamsa, the wicked king of Mathura who was afraid that, according to a prophecy, his nephew would kill him. **Mohan** took his mission of restoring the good-evil balance quite seriously and sent them all and many other demons packing. Let's check out some fearsome fiends who faced their end at the hands of the flute-playing **Kamsantaka**. (Erm, who are Mohan and Kamsantaka? Those are just two of the many names of Krishna. Some more have been underlined in this section. It would be interesting to do your own research about the meanings of these names.)*

PUTANA

When Kamsa realized that the infant **Shyam** had been smuggled out of prison, he sent his people to look for, locate and kill him. Putana, his faithful demon, went on a baby-killing spree, but **Murari** eluded her till she reached Braj. When she finally spotted him, she turned into a beautiful, loving woman and managed to get **Manohar** into her lap. She tried her usual modus operandi—feeding him her poisonous breast milk. Big mistake! The all-knowing **Sarvajana** knew exactly what was going on. He sucked out her life along with milk, and that was the end of Putana.

SHAKATASURA

When **Madhav** was barely twenty-seven days old, Shakatasura was sent to kill him. Yashoda had laid **Gopal** to sleep in the shade under a cart laden with pitchers of milk, curd and butter. What she didn't know was that the cart was a form assumed by the malicious Shakatasura! He pushed down with all his might to crush the dozing **Damodar** underneath. Unfortunately for him, the baby was incredibly strong and, with a single kick, shattered the cart—and the asura—into smithereens. From the reincarnation point of view, this was a fortunate event. In his previous birth, Shakatasura had been cursed to become bodiless, until touched by the foot of god.

TRINAVARTA

Kamsa's next goon was the formless demon Trinavarta. Once again, Yashoda had just laid **Balakrishna** to rest when the asura transformed into a massive whirlwind and swiftly rose into the sky, carrying the tot along, round and round, higher and higher, enveloping Gokul in blinding clouds of dust. As we know by now, **Nandagopala** was no ordinary kid. None of the chaos bothered him. He became heavier by the second, pushing Trinavarta down, and wrapped his chubby baby arms around Trinavarta's throat, sque-e-e-ezing harder and tighter till he choked and plunged lifeless to the ground, eyes popping out of his horrid head. **Anantajit** sat atop him, unharmed.

BAKASURA

Angered by Putana's death, her brother Bakasura took off to kill her killer. He assumed the form of a colossal crane and lay near Gokul's pastures with his beak wide open. When the cowherds came by, he grabbed **Shrikanta** in his beak and swallowed him. Terror-struck, the other *gopas* became breathless and fell unconscious. However, inside the demon's stomach, **Prajapati** was far from faint. He became a fireball and whirled round and round with such force that Bakasura had to puke his insides out. **Trivikrama** jumped out, grabbed the crane's beak and ripped him apart.

AGHASURA

The third sibling of Putana and Bakasura was now super angry with **Keshav**, and wanted revenge. He transformed into a humongous python and sat near the forest with his mouth open like a giant cave. While returning home after dusk, all the

cowherds and their cattle walked into this trap. **Madan** realized what had happened, and followed them right in. Once he'd trapped everyone inside, Aghasura tried to swallow them all in one gluttonous gulp, but **Jayant** had other plans. He inflated himself till the serpent started to choke, and then he became even bigger and bigger until Aghasura couldn't breathe and his head exploded.

DHENUKASURA

The terrible donkey demon Dhenukasura lived in Talavana, a forest full of palm trees. No one dared to enter the area to collect fruit, for they feared that the demon and his donkey troops would kill them. Of course, no such fear plagued **Jyotiraditya** and his brother Balarama, who led the hungry gopas straight in and shook the trees to knock down some tasty fruit. When Dhenukasura came hurtling at them, Balarama grabbed the demon by his tail and swung him round and round until his life exited. The donkey troops then came, thirsting for revenge, but were all struck down by **Sumedh**. Once again, the forest, with its sweet palm fruit, was open to all.

BANASURA

Thousand-armed Banasura, son of Prahlada, was a devotee of Shiva. His many hands came in rather handy when he played a mind-boggling number of drums to create amazing music while Shiva danced. Needless to say, Shiva gave him a boon of protection, but this made Banasura proud, haughty and quite cruel. No one could stand up to him, not even the devas. Now

his daughter Usha fell in love with and kidnapped Anirudha, grandson of **Jagadish**. This enraged **Sudarshana** so much that he came to battle Banasura, who promptly pinged Shiva for help. An epic duel ensued, and Shiva had to plead with **Purushottam** to spare his ward's life. **Chaturbhuja** agreed to this, but not before ordering his Sudarshana Chakra to chop off all but one pair of Banasura's arms. He also welcomed Usha into his family.

IN BUDDHIST MYTHOLOGY

MARA is one of the few 'villains' in the Buddhist tradition, often shown as a hideous demon and, at times, as an enormous elephant, bull or serpent. When shown as humanlike, he rides an elephant with extra tusks. Earlier in the book, you saw him as the demonic celestial king who teased and tempted Siddhartha, who was meditating to seek enlightenment. There are said

Read more about Mara in 'Call of Deity: Legendary Warfare', page 177.

to be many kinds of Maras including Klesha-Mara, Mrityu-Mara and Skandha-Mara, all of which attempt to upturn all that is good or make people do what is wrong. Some scholars believe that the name Mara is related to the term 'maya', which across the beliefs of Buddhism, Hinduism and even Sikhism is something that appears to be real, like this world, but is in fact just an illusion! It is possible that Mara was adapted from Namuci (or Namuchi),

a demon of darkness and drought featured in the Puranas. He threatens mankind as much by withholding the nurturing power of rain as by hiding the knowledge of truth. Interestingly, like Vritra, Namuci too was finally felled by foam.

KALAKEYAS or **KALAKANJAKAS,** vicious and awful-to-look-at *danavas* common to Hindu and Buddhist legend, lived at the bottom of a mammoth sea and emerged only at night to taunt and attack their targets: people, sages, devas. Because they were extremely powerful and because they would go hide in the waters, the devas couldn't get back at them. On Vishnu's advice, they asked Agastya to drink up the water—yes, all the water of the sea! When Agastya drained the sea, the Kalakeyas had no place to left to hide and were easily overcome. We wonder who refilled the sea.

IN ZOROASTRIAN MYTHOLOGY

AHRIMAN, the chief evil dude in Zoroastrian lore, is the opposite of Ahura Mazda. You have met both earlier in this book, locked in eternal combat. As dark is to light, night to day and stench to fragrance, so is Ahriman to Ahura Mazda. At the beginning of creation, Ahura Mazda recited the Ahuna Vairya prayer to defeat Ahriman, who responded by creating the deadly dragon Azi Dahaka, but then got scared of the horned-bull mace of Mithra, the deity of light, and fled. He ran away again when Zoroaster was born but returned to tempt the prophet, offering him the

kingdom of the world, if only he rejected the true faith. When Zoroaster refused, Ahriman despatched hordes of demons to attack him, but Zoroaster sent them all flying. In the final struggle, it is said that he will be defeated and reduced to nothingness.

AKA MANAH or **AKOMAN** is the demon of evil thoughts whose main purpose is to prevent people from doing what is right. He represents the opposite of Vohu Mano, who symbolizes 'good mind'. Akoman is considered a particularly dangerous demon as he can alter people's thoughts, making them forget how to tell the difference between right and wrong, and thus hurting others. He causes chaos and makes people miserable. In the final battle, he will fight Vohu Mano and be vanquished.

INDAR, another angry demon, has the power to freeze the minds of good people. Interestingly, he seems to have a few traits in common with Indra from the Rig Vedic tradition; both want sacrifices of animals and offerings of the elixir called soma or *haoma*. Indar is the foil to Asha Vahishta, the amesha spenta of truth and virtue.

NANGHAIT appears to be connected to the Ashwins, the horse-riding healer twins of Hinduism, though their helpful role has become rather hurtful in Zoroastrianism. The demon Nanghait is the arch-enemy of Armaiti, the goddess of gratitude, and insists on making people feel discontented with and ungrateful for what they have.

SAURVA or **SARWAR**, the demon of chaos and disease, is the main enemy of the amesha spenta Vairya, who protects paradise. Saurva too has a crossover connect, at times being identified, in an inverse manner, with Rudra or even Shiva from Hindu myth.

TAURIZ (or TAWRICH) and ZARIZ (or ZARICH) are both demonesses of Angra Mainyu. They started out as powerful spirits representing the natural world but, over time like fallen angels, they shifted focus on to the harmful aspects of their power. Tauriz is the demoness of destruction, opposed to Haurvatat, goddess of wholeness. By symbolizing ageing as well as poison—both the antitheses of life—Zariz counters Ameretat, goddess of immortality.

AESHMA, a truly evil and brutal stooge of Ahriman, turns all good things upside down with the force of anger. His name means 'fury'. His chief adversary is the protector yazata Sraosha, who is Ahura Mazda's messenger and works through the power of prayer and discipline. Three times every night, he descends to Earth to crush the skulls of demons that harass men. It is believed that Sraosha will overthrow Aeshma at the end of the world.

NASU, demoness of dead stuff, lives in hell. As soon as she hears that someone has died, she emerges from the darkness in the form of a fly, and tries to contaminate the corpse before the funeral. She symbolizes decay, so it can also be said that she helps in decomposition. Yet she is considered the world's greatest polluter. The only thing that scares her is a 'four-eyed' dog, one that has a spot above each eye.

IN ABRAHAMIC (CHRISTIAN, JEWISH, ISLAMIC) MYTHOLOGIES

IBLIS, originally an angel and said to be closest to God, refused to bow to Adam even when God commanded. As punishment, he was cast out of heaven and has since become the Devil, or the tempter. He and his spirits, called jinns, shall be punished after the Day of Judgement, till when they are allowed to play their games with all but the true believers. They have no real power over people but can only tempt them with evil suggestions. Iblis is said to be the actual name of as-Shaitan, equivalent to Satan in Christian lore.

SATAN, the Devil and arch-enemy of God, tried to spoil all of God's works to lure his followers away from the path of righteousness, even to tempt Christ during his meditation in the wilderness. In Judaism, Satan is a metaphor for the tendency inside us humans to do wrong, to be nasty, to err. Across Abrahamic religions, Satan ranks below God in terms of power and ability. He is more an irritant—although a serious one—than a really worthwhile opponent. He is also called Lucifer, or Light-Bringer.

LILITH was actually the first woman, created by God from the same clay and at the same time as Adam. When God told her to serve Adam, she refused (seems to have been a trend!), claiming that they were equals. Yay women power! Well, she too was cast out of Eden. While God made another woman, Eve, this time using parts of Adam, Lilith became a demon who preys on

unmarried men, children and pregnant women. Interestingly, in Sumerian legend, Lilitu are a group of troublesome wind spirits who attack children and women.

HARUT AND MARUT were originally angels too, noble and pure. They saw the evils of men on Earth and scoffed. When God challenged them to behave better in the same situations, they took up the dare. Alas, they too ended up getting tempted to lie, cheat and kill, even better (or worse?) than humans. Realizing their folly but not wanting eternal damnation, they chose to be punished on Earth and were hung upside down in a well in Babylon. They will remain suspended there till the world ends, their thirsty tongues sticking out but unable to reach the water, which is just the thickness-of-a-sword-blade away . . . Ah, tantalizing, like the myth of Tantalus! The names Harut and Marut could be distortions of Haurvatat and Ameretat.

To refresh your memory, flip back to 'Gods of All Things', page 34.

SOLUTIONS

CHAPTER 1

W	A	Y	A	M	E	L	O	H	I	M	T	A
S	A	M	S	A	R	A	M	A	E	O	H	H
W	O	G	A	Y	O	M	A	R	T	U	M	R
A	L	O	Y	H	A	V	W	O	N	N	Z	I
Y	G	L	W	O	R	F	L	A	V	T	B	N
A	N	D	B	S	H	I	V	A	G	A	P	A
M	E	E	H	R	N	A	M	H	A	R	B	M
B	Q	N	U	A	I	R	D	A	R	A	H	S
H	H	X	C	R	T	E	W	T	N	F	Z	A
U	F	E	Y	N	S	I	H	Q	E	A	C	T
Z	I	A	W	W	A	H	H	W	W	T	Z	A
A	M	A	N	H	A	R	B	S	A	M	H	Z
N	A	S	A	D	I	Y	A	S	U	K	T	A
U	R	U	G	E	H	A	W	A	D	T	M	Y

WORDS IN THE MAZE: 1. GAYOMART; 2. HAWWA; 3. MOUNT ARAFAT; 4. SHIVA; 5. AHRIMAN; 6. SAMSARA; 7. WAHEGURU; 8. YAZATAS; 9. SWAYAMBHU; 10. GOLDEN; 11. ELOHIM; 12. AHUNA VAIRYA; 13. BRAHMAN; 14. NASADIYA SUKTA; 15. TUSHITA

CHAPTER 2

WHO'S WHO? (in order of appearance): Kartikeya; Saraswati; Agni; Manjushri; Haurvatat and Ameretat

CHAPTER 3
A MAP OF MYTHS

¹K	A	I	L	A	¹¹S	H					
	²V	I	S	H	**W**	A	K	A	R	M	A
				³V	**A**	I	K	U	N	T	H	A
		⁴A	M	A	**R**	A	V	A	T	I	
		⁵G	A	N	**G**	R	I	N	P	O	C	H	E
	⁶S	A	T	Y	**A**	L	O	K	A		
	⁷P	A	T	A	**L**	A					
		⁸N	A	R	**O**	B	O	N	C	H	U	N	G
			⁹R	A	**K**	S	H	A	S	T	A	L
		¹⁰V	I	Z	**A**	R	E	S	H		

LIVING LEGENDS: (1) Manikaran (Himachal Pradesh); (2) Hanuman (son of Anjana); (3) Dronagiri; (4) Pachmarhi; (5) Rozabal

CHAPTER 4

CROSSWORD SOLUTION: (1) (Across) MAKARDHWAJA; (Down) MARKANDEYA; (2) ELEPHANT; (3) JAMADAGNI; (4) MUCHKUNDA; (5) ONAM; (6) DRONAGIRI; (7) KRIPACHARYA; (8) BHARGAVA; (9) SAHADEVA; (10) SARAMA; (11) JAMBAVAN; (12) VED VYASA; (13) KAG BHUSHUNDI

CHAPTER 5

	¹B	O	D	H	I	⁸S	A	T	T	V	A
	²N	A	R	A	S	I	M	H	A		
	³P	A	N	C	H	A	J	A	N	Y	A
	⁴A	S	H	W	A	M	E	D	H	A	
		⁵K	A	I	K	E	Y	I			
⁶Z	A	R	A	T	H	U	S	T	R	A	
			⁷U	P	E	K	K	H	A		

MATCHED PAIRS: Ahura Mazda (E); Ashwins (D); Parinirvana (B); Jaya and Vijaya (A); Yin and Yang (F); Damian and Cosmas (C)

CHAPTER 6
NAME GAME: Agni: Ram; Vayu: Antelope; Yamuna: Tortoise; Ganga: Makara; Bhairava: Dog; Ayyappan: Tiger; Budh: Yali; Shani: Crow; Kamadeva: Parrot; Shitala: Donkey

MINI QUIZ: (1) d. Valaha; (2) c. Vasuki; (3) a. Staff of Musa; (4) a. Sharabha; (5) b. Kalki; (6) d. Chamrosh

CHAPTER 7
MISSING TREE NAMES: BANYAN; COCONUT; TULSI; ANKOL; RUDRAKSHA; MANGO

CROSSWORD SOLUTION: (1) CYPRESS; (2) MYRTLE;
(3) KHEJARI; (4) (Across) BURNING BUSH; (Down) BARESMAN;
(5) BRAMBLE; (6) CEDAR; (7) BONBIBI; (8) BHAWANI;
(9) SANJEEVANI; (10) MARJORAM; (11) KETAKI

CHAPTER 8
WORDS IN THE WORM: (1) VEDAS; (2) SUTTAS; (3)
SAMHITA; (4) ADI GRANTH; (5) HADITH; (6) HOTRI; (7) INJIL;
(8) LAWGIVER; (9) REVELATION; (10) NIYAMSARA;
(11) AVESTA; (12) ABHIDHAMMA; (13) ATONEMENT;
(14) TIPITAKA; (15) ARANYAKA; (16) ARABIC; (17) CHOLA;
(18) APOSTLES; (19) SATKHANDAGAMA; (20) ATHARVA

CHAPTER 9
BATTLE FORMATIONS: 1-E; 2-C; 3-F; 4-G; 5-A; 6-H; 7-B; 8-D

CHAPTER 10
CROSSWORD SOLUTION: (1) GANDIVA; (2) TVASHTAR;
(3) BRAHMASHIRSHA; (4) NAGAPASHA; (5) NARAYANASTRA;
(6) CHANDRAHASA; (7) KARTIKEYA; (8) (ACROSS) PINAKA;
(DOWN) PASHUPATA; (9) SHAKTI; (10) DADHEECHI;
(11) SUDARSHANA

GUESS THE WEAPON: (1) Mace; (2) Sword; (3) Plough; (4) Spear

GOD AND WEAPON PAIRS: (1) Kartikeya + (C) Vel;
(2) Parashurama + (A) Parashu; (3) Ravana + (D) Chandrahasa;
(4) Kali + (B) Khadaga

CHAPTER 11

WHAT'S THE CONNEQT?: Bhima: Sutasoma (son of Draupadi); Shiva: Kartikeya (Hindu god of war); Arjuna: Abhimanyu (son of Subhadra); Shantanu: Bhishma (son of River Ganga); Hiranyakashipu: Prahlada; Uttanapada: Dhruva (personification of the North Star); Rama: Lav-Kush (twins born in Valmiki's ashram); Yayati: Puru (ancestor of Pandavas and Kauravas)

CHAPTER 12

WORDS IN THE WORM: (1) ONAM; (2) MAHALAYA; (3) ABHISHEK; (4) KAMADEVA; (5) ARGHYA; (6) ATTUKAL; (7) LOSAR; (8) RATH YATRA; (9) ANANT; (10) TSECHU; (11) UGADI; (12) INDRASENAN; (13) NAVREH; (14) HOLA MOHALLA; (15) ADITYAHRIDAYAM; (16) MODAK; (17) KAGYED; (18) DHULENDI; (19) INDRADHWAJA; (20) ASTRA PUJA

ORDER OF NUGGETS: 7, 13, 1, 2, 15, 6, 9, 12, 20, 18, 4, 8, 3, 11, 16, 5, 14, 17, 10, 19

ACKNOWLEDGEMENTS

Many energies converged to nurture *Mythonama*, and we acknowledge their inspirational generosity with deep gratitude.

All our lives, our families have shared with us wonderful tales, timeless or invented in a jiffy, making us curious to know more and keen to share more. We are happy to transmit this intangible legacy.

India's mythologies, bridging multiple religious beliefs and folklores, present a fascinating labyrinth, a leela played out in fantastic tales of heroism and hubris. The deeper we delve, the more intricate the patterns, the richer our insights . . . Several bright young minds worked with us through this maze of research and structuring: Siddhartha Kurapati, Shireen Mubayi, Kirti Gupta and Manpreet Shoora. Thank you all for helping us not lose the thread! Ibtesam Rahman and Noor Mubayi read our drafts with Arjuna-like focus, weeding out errors and inconsistencies and suggesting improvements. Thank you, both!

Mythonama would still be a myth but for the incredible professionalism of the Puffin team. Arpita Nath guided this book's journey with her signature blend of candid optimism and publishing acumen. Aditi Batra's thorough, objective editing

transformed it from manuscript to book, while Canato Jimo and Doodlenerve (Subhadeep Roy and Shiladitya Bose) interpreted it so imaginatively to give it this gorgeous visual avatar. We love it!

A loud shout-out also to Niyati Dhuldhoya, with whom we conceptualized this book years ago, and to the Puffin sales and marketing teams for their stellar efforts in making this book reach the readers it is written for.